Sir Winston Churchill

Sir Winston Churchill

MASTER OF COURAGE

Princess Marthe Bibesco

THE JOHN DAY COMPANY   *New York*

FIRST AMERICAN EDITION 1959

TRANSLATED FROM THE FRENCH BY VLADIMIR KEAN

Library of Congress Catalogue
Card Number: 59-7122

MANUFACTURED IN THE UNITED STATES OF AMERICA

"Facts are better than dreams"

WINSTON CHURCHILL

10 May 1940

Contents

Sir Winston Churchill

Part One

IN PRAISE OF COURAGE

ERASMUS, whose famous portrait in the Louvre makes him look so wise, proved his wisdom by writing *In Praise of Folly*; folly is indispensable, if for no other purpose than to confound those men who delude themselves that they are actuated by reason and therefore proceed to commit the incredible number of stupid blunders recorded throughout history. This is clearly shown in those absurd manuals which pass as textbooks in which the same stories are repeated century after century and, in the newspapers, from day to day. "He who eschews folly is lacking in wisdom," writes a French moralist; but today to live without courage would be even more insane than to live without folly, if such a thing were humanly possible. It is impossible to have enough courage; we all need it, every sort, kind and variety of courage, according to our characters and circumstances; we need courage every day of our lives. In order to live with some measure of happiness and to be able to overcome our personal difficulties, we need help from the great masters of courage; among them, Churchill shines with particular brilliance.

This "professor of energy," as Barrès would have called him, has made courage the most exciting of sports, and raised it not only to the dignity of a profession but even to the level of a work of art. He has chosen it as a calling, superior to all others. It can be recognized as the only possible choice, whatever difficulties it involved.

Watching his progress throughout his career I have often asked myself what was the secret of his fascination for all and sundry. Everyone who comes in contact with him feels it and there is every reason to believe that he is not immune to it himself. There is an element of dry humor in this, as he has never had any illusions about himself and has faced the fact that he is a phenomenon, from his youth upwards. What a spectacle his life provides! Has there ever been an actor-playwright who has had a greater capacity for "putting over" his own personality? No man has shunned the public eye less than he has; everybody knows him or thinks he knows him. There is no mystery about him. He hides nothing, has never wittingly deceived anybody; and, when he has made mistakes, could anybody, later, admit the fact more candidly than he? He has demonstrated the three essential forms of courage: courage to risk his own life without hesitation; courage to displease others and defy their opinions; courage to love a cause better than himself.

These three forms are only an introduction to a catalogue of his many and sometimes apparently contradictory forms of courage: the courage to admit that he is wrong and proclaim it out loud; for example he wrote referring to the end of 1939: "Our ambassador in Athens was right and I was wrong"; the courage to attack and criticize an adversary pitilessly without descending to the level of base insults, and then only when his enemy is riding the crest of a wave. This was exemplified in his reply to Stalin in Moscow reproaching him for his attacks and abuse: "That was when you were against us." He has, too, the courage to adopt other people's ideals, expressed for example in his unbounded admiration for French military prowess, his fetishism for Napoleon, for Clemenceau. So sincere is this admiration that he actually wept in public when the French Military Medal was conferred upon him.

Also his is the courage to admit that he has a craving for power; the courage to relinquish it, not only when forced to do so by others, which is easy seeing that it is inevitable, but of his own accord, which requires great courage; the courage to identify himself completely with his people during the years of their great trial; then, he became their only voice, their only effective gesture, their only countenance—and the people had such faith in him that they invested him with powers comparable to those of Prometheus. It was Prometheus who, when chained to the rock for stealing Fire, revealed to the Oceanides the secret of the only remedy he had been able to find to save the condemned race of man: "I filled their hearts with blind hope."

PORTRAIT OF CHURCHILL—A PRELIMINARY SKETCH

This great man can never be ignored by historians. His actions are subject to criticism and discussion, as is the case with every human being; adept at attacking and defending himself, he has been hated, loved, suspected, antagonized, scoffed at, extolled, idolized in turn, and then betrayed, like other men whose exceptional gifts have made them greater than their fellows. But it would be invidious to deny that Churchill is one of the greatest of Englishmen, dead or alive. He saved England by his grim determination, his passionate devotion, and his absolute faith in the character of the English people.

I have known Winston Churchill since my own early youth, and in making this preliminary sketch of a portrait I have been able to outline a sufficient number of characteristic features, observed by myself or others, to enable me to do without a formal sitting as it were, or the use of photographs. What I shall try to do, in order to present a composite portrait of his personality with its gestures and expressions, is compile an album of snapshots taken either by friends who knew him before I did, by close relatives, by his own friends and collaborators, by his adversaries, by his predecessors and successors, or by myself.

It is generally recognized that a precocious genius experiences great difficulty in overcoming the incredulity and obstruction arrayed against him. But what could be more tragic for an ambitious young man than the skepticism and lack of appreciation of an illustrious family? Especially when his own father, Lord Randolph Churchill, younger brother of the Duke of Marlborough, was considered a great statesman and the future leader of a regenerated Conservative Party by everybody, friend or foe, who had heard him speak in the House of Commons. His mother, one of the reigning beauties of London, paid court to by the Prince of Wales, surrounded by admiration and flattery, was the celebrated Miss Jennie Jerome —the first of those young heiresses from the New World who came over to the Old World to conquer it with their new weapons of intrepid youth and beauty. He was born at Blenheim, the palace of his grandfather, the Duke of Marlborough, one festive night amidst merrymaking. His mother reluctantly tore herself away from the ballroom only after he had made his impatience to come into this world known by the most obvious signs. He was born in a dressing room; Winston had arrived before Lady Randolph had time to reach her bedroom!

Throughout his early childhood he was the apple of discord and the object of rivalry between his mother's and his father's families; he was born under contradictory stars. His mother had American ideas about bringing up children; his grandmother, the redoubtable Duchess of Marlborough, who at that time still reigned over Blenheim, had different ideas in keeping with the best British traditions. The beautiful Jennie, whose amber complexion gave rise to rumors of a drop of Indian blood, was too busy

15

enjoying the intoxicating experience of a successful woman of fashion to play at being a devoted mother. His father, Lord Randolph, was entirely absorbed in two things: his politics, which were good, and his health which, unfortunately, was bad. But the little boy, with his brooding, almost sulky expression, with his blue eyes lit from time to time by strange flashes of intelligence, who might one day, God's will, be master of Blenheim, was no sooner out of his cradle and planted on his own two feet than he came under the influence of his mother's American family, who unceasingly fought against his dominating grandmother. There were three Jerome sisters, all beautiful and attractive, though very different. The second, Leonie, was Jennie's favorite. She later became Lady Leslie, married in England to Sir John Leslie, of Irish extraction. He was an efficient officer, later attached to the court as military attaché to the Duke of Connaught, the youngest son of Queen Victoria, who was to become Governor-General of Canada.

Leonie, his young aunt, took the child under her wing in order to keep him away from his grandmother, whenever Lady Randolph had to go away during parliamentary recesses, either to the South of France, to shoot in Scotland, or on a cruise in the Mediterranean—and soon, alas, because the health of her brilliant husband became rapidly worse.

Lord Randolph was still young enough when he died for everyone to say that "if he had lived" he would inevitably have become the leader of his Party and Prime Minister, that he was the greatest orator of his time, and that England had buried the only man capable of saving the Conservative Party and, consequently, the Empire! Young Winston's first battle was against the shadow of his father, a battle which was to prove extremely difficult to win. It started at his preparatory school. Lord Randolph was a brilliant scholar, his son proved to be his exact opposite; he was at the bottom of his class and hated by his fellow pupils who ganged up against him; he was bullied unmercifully. He defended himself bravely but was overwhelmed by the weight of numbers. Wild with rage, incensed by the cowardice of the pack, and already conscious of his own valor—the secret of which he was dimly conscious—he shouted: "Cowards! I will make you pay for this! I shall be Prime Minister one day and I will get even with all of you."

How could he be so certain of his destiny? Nobody knows. On one occasion, during the Christmas holidays, the two families quarreled over him with particular acrimony. His father and mother had left on a cruise which was to hasten Lord Randolph's convalescence but which ended in his death. The Duchess of Marlborough, his grandmother, wanted him to come to Blenheim. But before leaving, his mother had entrusted him to her favorite sister, Leonie, in whom Jennie had complete confidence; young and jolly herself, with several children of her own, Leonie knew how to amuse them and give them a good time. She lived in London and knew everything there was to be known about theatres and circuses. Many years later, when Winston was recognized as a great man and every family memento was considered a precious relic,

Seymour, Leonie's son, showed me a letter in which Grandmother made a pressing appeal, tantamount to an order to Leonie to send him to Blenheim for Christmas. The duchess complained bitterly that her daughter-in-law, though ill-advised enough to be afraid of the cold and the drafts in a palace in winter, was sure to neglect the danger of infectious microbes—whooping cough, scarlet fever, and German measles—which naturally infested all the London theatres; especially at Christmastime when thousands of schoolchildren, neglected by their parents, badly dressed, badly behaved, all running at the nose, flocked to these badly ventilated places to see the pantomimes which are the special delight of young Londoners. The children were all bound to be contaminated. The letter and the appeal failed; the recipient was not convinced. The duchess was not to have her grandson at Blenheim for Christmas. Nothing could be done, it was a scandal! By this time Winston had become more of a nephew to Leonie than he was grandson to the duchess. He was to have his fill of pantomimes, stamp his feet when the curtain rose and immerse himself in the performance with the enthusiasm of a born actor. Even as a little boy he appreciated the pleasures of the theatre to the full, the performance and the crowded audience, the lights, the noise and the applause! He was born to live in public, he could already see himself on the stage, he imagined himself across the footlights, jumping on the stage and being the hero of the play! Meanwhile he was an utter failure at school.

He did not qualify for a university; even the largest colleges rejected him—that was not to be his fate. He would don the Oxford mortar board with its golden tassel only when he was made doctor *honoris causa.* Like Bonaparte after his return from the campaign in Italy, he was also to become a member of the Institut de France. But all that was then still wrapped in the mists of the future. His school would be the school of life, organized and entirely created by him. As soon as he had embraced one career he was eager to change it. His life is an unbroken sequence of experiences.

Like many young English aristocrats, he decided to join the army. After going to Sandhurst he was sent to the cavalry. Examinations, mathematics, trigonometry, were not his strong points; but a regiment of Hussars, the Queen's Own, what bliss! And to charge, sword flashing in the air! That was his dream! His period of training seemed all too short, but it was a happy period. Cavalry meant, in England as it did in India, polo.

He had a passion for polo, but what really attracted him was fighting, of which competitive sport was merely a foretaste. He had a craving for the firing line, for his baptism of fire. His first exploit was characteristic—there was fighting in Cuba. The Spaniards were defending the last fragments of that immense empire, on which the sun never set, against the United States. Young Winston, dreaming epic dreams, volunteered; he was supposed to go to Cuba as a war correspondent, but, in his case, that was merely the pretext. Winston had decided that he

19

would go and fight for Spain. His first campaign, his first passage of arms, was to be against America, his mother's country. Later, in his speech to the American Congress in the middle of the second World War, he was to say: "If my father had been American and my mother British instead of the other way round I might have got here on my own." Americans bear him no grudge; they have adopted him and have already put an inscription to his glory on the house in which his mother was born. And the Jeromes pride themselves on being responsible, to the extent of fifty per cent, for the creation of this extraordinary scion of the house of Marlborough. One of his thousand biographers will write: "Churchill is fifty per cent American and sixty per cent English."

In fact, he was destined to fight against and on the side of his atavistic strains, for and against his heredity; he was conceived for one purpose only and he himself would be the first to proclaim his conviction of the fact: to fight. And when it becomes his fate to fight against adversity, against an enemy stronger than his friends, against bad luck and bad faith, against stupidity, against complacency, against the egotism of the powers that be, against the inertia of the weak, against everybody, when everything is against him and everything is going as badly as possible in the worst of possible worlds, then and only then will he be certain that he is going to be supremely happy! He is buoyed up by a presentiment of his splendid future. Chateaubriand would have said of him, as he said about the Other One, to whom Churchill has always, in the privacy of his own thoughts, compared himself:

"But Napoleon's destiny, like all great destinies, was a muse. . . ."

When the fortunes of England were at their lowest ebb in South Africa, young Churchill hastened to join the fray, pen in one hand (in his capacity as war correspondent), rifle in the other, like the born fighter he has always been. He was taken prisoner by the Boers, but he managed to escape. His destiny could not be fulfilled inside a barbed-wire compound; he was fated to be an expert at escaping from everything, outside all rules and conventions, away from the stereotyped situation! His political career began, as his military career had, in a burst of glory. Was it not a fact that his father had not lived long enough to rejuvenate the members of the Conservative Party? Very well, he would rejuvenate them, in a very different fashion. How? Quite simply, by becoming a Liberal. Political parties, like the planets, usually gravitate from left to right, and the same applies to the members of these parties. When one has been unfortunate enough to be born on the right, with one's nose against the wall, why not say Where shall I go? Winston, characteristically, escaped by a short cut; but like the prodigal son, he went away in order to stage a magnificent comeback and stayed away just long enough to give the father time to prepare the fatted calf. By temperament Winston is a Liberal, a democrat, and a man of the left; his enemies would call him a demagogue; he is instinctively generous to others. He is a man of hot passions. Fashionable drawing-room gatherings made no provision for the passions. The Liberals dreamed of great reforms and their clubs welcomed imaginative thinkers. When Churchill became a Cabinet Minister for the first time, it was in a Liberal government, presided over by Asquith, who appointed him First Lord of the Admiralty.

A short time ago in London, a group of us were comparing notes about the man and somebody suggested the following game: each one in turn was to say where, and under what circumstances, he had first met Winston Churchill. The first to be asked was Lady Violet Bonham Carter, Asquith's eldest daughter. I asked her if their first meeting had taken place at Downing Street where she was then living with her father. She thought for a moment and said: "No, the first time I saw him was in London at a dinner party. I was sitting next to him. He did not open his mouth. He was hunched up with his head down between his shoulders and seemed to be brooding about something. He intimidated me and I was piqued because he would not talk to me, so I said nothing; then I decided to start a conversation with the man on the other side of me, who was only too delighted. Because I was annoyed and wanted to annoy Winston, I kept up the conversation for a long time. All the time I was talking to the man on my right I had the curious impression that something like a banked-up fire was smoldering on my left. Just before the end of dinner, Winston Churchill turned toward me and said suddenly, in that chuckling voice of his which we all know, 'How old are you?' I answered, 'Nineteen.'

"'Ah,' he cried, 'and to think that I am thirty-eight! Already thirty-eight! My life is finished! Is it worth going on living when one has lost one's youth?' And he launched out on a prodigious improvisation on the hackneyed theme of the shortness of life, how little time was vouchsafed to the miserable human race; but these commonplace platitudes were transformed by his eloquence; it was a dazzling display of oratory. As a spent fireworks rocket falls to the ground, he relapsed into silence. Then he raised his head and concluded:

" 'We are all nothing but worms, miserable worms!' " Then, with a defiant air, but with a malicious gleam in his eye:

" 'Yes, nothing but worms, miserable worms, but I, you see, I intend to be . . . and shall be . . . a glowworm!' "

My turn came next: The first time I set eyes on this "glowworm," who acted as his own prophet, was in Paris, at lunch in the Marquis de Breteuil's private house in the spring of 1914. Churchill was at that time First Lord of the Admiralty in Asquith's Cabinet. Our host had invited several members of the French parliament to meet the man responsible for giving orders to the Grand Fleet, which was then making sure that communication between England and France would not be interfered with while the storm was brewing beyond the Rhine. Among others, there was Aristide Briand, who was then Garde des Sceaux (equivalent to Lord Privy Seal) and Jules Roche, whose enthusiastic support for the Entente Cordiale was well known. All the Frenchmen present were either in lounge suits or frock coats, out of respect for the foreign guest. Churchill alone wore a dark "veston" suit with a bow tie, askew as usual, and he seemed impatient. He kept darting searching glances around the room. Which of these men, invited to this political lunch party organized by our host in order to further the Entente Cordiale, would give him the information he was looking for? What did they think he stood for? He was a Liberal and a minister in the Asquith Government, but was that enough to inspire confidence in Briand, the Socialist, who was said to be the man who had promised to blow up the sewers on the "great night"? In the minds of all Frenchmen, Churchill was associated with the shadow of the Grand Fleet; a redoubtable shadow athwart the exaggerated ambitions of William II, which by this time were common knowledge in all the chancelleries. . . . April 1914! Jules Cambon, the French Ambassador at Berlin, had been warning the Quai d'Orsay throughout the preceding year; King Albert had given detailed information to the French government; Alphonso XIII had spoken to Marshal Lyautey; such men as Poincaré, Philippe Berthelot, Paul Cambon, Paléologue, were all convinced of it. The Emperor wanted war—it was an open secret.

I was watching Churchill from the other side of the table. This was the first time I had seen that powerful mask, like the face of a white bulldog or a genial clown, "this powdered lump of flesh so fearsome to his enemies." Thanks to the congenital pallor of the redhead, it seemed lit from within like a globe of alabaster. When at rest, it is massive and brooding, the mouth tightly closed, like a gash made with an engraving tool, fixed in an expression of contempt because he has had to answer so many in-

24

IN PRAISE OF COURAGE

credibly stupid questions. That was how he appeared to me on that day and the memory has never left me.

At the Marquis de Breteuil's table the conversation became general as soon as the meal started, as is usual in France. This served to plunge Churchill even more deeply into silence. He had exchanged a few words of conventional politeness in English with his hostess, who was almost a countrywoman of his. The gentle, white-haired Marquise de Breteuil, resembling one of those faded figures in an eighteenth-century pastel, was American. Afterwards he preserved an obstinate silence, but I sensed that he was quite at his ease; he was eating and drinking with relish everything that was put in front of him and, obviously, was not missing a word of the conversation around him. Monsieur de Breteuil, noticing this silence, which might seem sulky to anyone who did not know him—actually in Churchill's case it is the outward sign of extreme concentration—and might well give offense to the other guests, began to act as an interpreter for the Frenchman who was particularly anxious to make Churchill talk. It was Jules Roche who started the ball rolling: Was it a fact that the Liberals had promised to introduce new agrarian laws into Ireland, as they had into England? Were these laws going to be submitted to Parliament? Was it not true that they were of such a nature that they might well disorganize production throughout the country? Would this not be a source of embarrassment to the government? Churchill tucked his head still farther down between his shoulders and shrugged them;

he had been round before and now he was square, like a Picasso drawing. He grunted a few words—in English, no doubt—between his teeth, which nobody could understand. Breteuil amiably volunteered to amplify and translate Jules Roche's ideas and did so at some length. Churchill remained silent. Was he deaf, or, perhaps, was he embarrassed? Actually, he was getting ready, like a spring he was coiling himself before letting fly.

Aristide Briand, in his melodious voice, made an attempt to steer the discussion, which had begun so inauspiciously, into smoother waters. "In fact," said the French Minister of Justice, "you are trying to introduce into England the system of small rural properties which we have had in France ever since the Revolution, am I right?"

Then, the Churchill catapult leaped into action. "No," he said firmly, in tolerably correct French, "no, not that, not that at all! What we are aiming at in England . . . is collective state property!" When he had finished speaking, his head, which he had raised for a moment, sank back into its usual place between his shoulders. It was then, during the ensuing moments of astonished silence, that I caught a glimpse, for the first time, of that will-o'-the-wisp shining in his eyes; that little flame, that glint like a dancing spark, which can always be interpreted as a signal that the action is about to begin.

When lunch was over we had coffee in the library, beneath the full-length portrait of Louis XVI presented by the monarch to the Baron of Breteuil, last ambassador of the King of France at Constantinople, before 1793. Churchill came and sat beside me. He seemed relaxed and told me that he was to visit Saint-Cyr immediately after lunch; he was naturally impatient to be off! He was, as ever, spoiling for the fight! He could detect the familiar smell of powder and danger. He was impatient because he was in a hurry to meet those young men who were going to fight and die, rather than linger around the table in the company of men who were going to live long enough to see their political illusions swept away one by one. Much as I was longing to do so, I could not summon up the courage to ask him the reason for his extraordinary sally. Was it simply because he took malicious pleasure in disconcerting or even shocking his audience? Or was it because he wanted to show that he was further to the left than a French Socialist wished him to be, or even than the Moderates expected? They were liable to consider him a reactionary, a wolf in sheep's clothing, or one of those warriors hidden inside the Trojan horse. Or might it not simply have been his taste for paradoxes, or the Englishman's distaste for serious conversation around the luncheon table, where he prefers to forget politics, relax and talk about anything under the sun except what concerns him when he sits at the council table? I was to wait five years for an answer.

I saw Churchill again on many occasions during and after the war, first in London, at his mother's, at his aunt Leonie Leslie's house, but more often in the country, where we had many friends in common.

First I shall tell when and why the question came back to my mind, that question which I had asked myself and which had remained unanswered for five years. It was in May 1919. I was sitting next to Winston Churchill at dinner in his mother's house; now or never was the time to remind him of our first talk: "What made you say to those French deputies, at the Breteuil lunch in April 1914, that in England you were aiming at collective state property?" He took his time before answering; the will-o'-the-wisp was dancing in his eye: "Very simple, I wanted to astonish them . . . because they thought that I was behind the times and a reactionary. . . ."

Each time I met Churchill again the circumstances seemed exceptional, but never so much so as on one occasion when, by an extraordinary coincidence, I found myself, at the right time and place, walking with Winston on the white cliffs which dominate Dover and Folkestone. From there on a fine day the coast of France can be glimpsed, a faint line that is a different blue from the blue of the sky or the sea.

It was sunset on the last day of July. We walked in silence, breathing in deeply the sea air and the smell of the salt-impregnated fields. Suddenly Winston Churchill stood still and pointed his cane toward the horizon. "Exactly seven years ago, to the very day, I ordered the Grand Fleet to proceed from the North Sea to the Channel! And I had no right to do so! No right, without having consulted the Cabinet. And I had no intention of consulting it . . ." The will-o'-the-wisp was shining merrily in his eyes. He added: "Afterwards I informed the Prime Minister, who informed the Cabinet. I had no right to do so, but I did it all the same!" He had said all this just like a little boy determined to have his own way, whether the authorities above him liked it or not.

We sat down on the grass for a while and contemplated the scene of his memorable deed, which was now deserted. It was here that the vessels of the Home Fleet, all lights extinguished, steamed past on that never-to-be-forgotten and decisive night. The fleet had been ordered to disperse after the North Sea maneuvers. But the counter-order arrived: instead of separating, the Grand Fleet steamed from the North Sea to the Channel. Winston had taken the entire responsibility on his own shoulders, without consulting his Cabinet colleagues! But the passage between France and England was barred to the German fleet for the duration of the war.

That day, once again, Winston Churchill had broken the mold and conquered, irrespective of rules and conventions. That is genius. Act according to instinct, as if the event had left you time for reflection. Act first and folly becomes wisdom. . . .

Knowing how fond Leonie Leslie was first of the child and then of the young man whom she had watched grow up, piling contradiction on contradiction, hurtling more than once toward what seemed inevitable downfall, criticized and discussed, first by his own family and then publicly, I sometimes said to tease her: "When will your nephew Winston become Prime Minister?"

Her reply was: "Never, except in the event of a catastrophe!"

As catastrophes never fail to fall upon us, Churchill became Prime Minister: "From defeat to defeat, from disaster to disaster, from catastrophe to catastrophe, right up to the final victory!"

Leonie died before she could witness what she never for a moment doubted—her nephew's capacity to rise above the cyclone and dominate it.

Everybody knows the rest of it. But a short sentence from his war memoirs is particularly revealing—it shows his most extraordinary quality, his reaction to misfortune which, in him, takes the form of contentment, a sort of expansive happiness. He had accepted the supreme responsibility at the hour of England's direst peril, when the British people, sorely stricken, threatened with extermination, felt its nation's very foundations crumbling. It was the 10th of May 1940. Upon returning from Buckingham Palace after swearing the oath of allegiance to the King (Chamberlain's ministry had been replaced by that presided over by Winston Churchill), he wrote: *Although impatient for the morning I slept soundly and had no need for cheering dreams. Facts are better than dreams.*

He was now Prime Minister, an office which his father, Lord Randolph, had never filled. He was head of a government which included both Tories and Labour. He had made a private vow to save England and he believed that he had been put on earth for the purpose of saving it. After which, he slept peacefully. He believed that he was strong enough to bend destiny to his will. Like Alexander when the Delphic Sibyl proved recalcitrant, he would

30

have her dragged by the hair in front of her tripod and force her to prophesy as he wished. It is then that the cry will be wrung from her lips which has echoed down the ages: "Oh! my son, thou art invincible!"

THE COURAGE OF CHILDHOOD

WINSTON CHURCHILL has remained a child throughout his life. The more usual tendency is for children to want to grow up, to anticipate the inevitable and to believe that they are inferior, humiliated and restricted as long as they have not crossed the boundary of puberty. But the child who realizes that he is worth more than any grownup, that he is nearer to God, that his knowledge is in every way superior to that of adults, that his instinct is nearly as sure as that of the animals, that child will be saved. Churchill makes a pretense of being a man; he will become, like everybody else, a terrifying adolescent, and then a young man with an expression of profound wisdom, then the man, overweight with something of a paunch, and finally the great, unforgettable personality. But never for an instant has he denied the fact of which he is so deeply conscious: his childhood has never left him. It is not dead, but merely sleeping; it will wake up at the most trifling excuse. In spite of himself, in spite of the inexorable passage of time, in spite of the years of apprenticeship at school, in spite of the masters and his fellow pupils (equally hated by him), his childhood sticks to his skin and his soul, it will never leave him.

One day, taken by surprise by the triteness of a remark, he found the answer to his own enigma in one of those blinding flashes of intuition which illuminate and reveal. One of those important ladies who haunt public ceremonies and invariably attend the baptism of their friends' babies said, intending to pay him a compliment as she leaned over the cradle of Winston II, "My dear Prime Minister! What an extraordinary likeness, he is the image of you!" "That is true," replied Churchill, "but, you know, all babies look like me!"

Throughout his life he has given proof of this essential childishness. In repose, his expression is serious, just like a newborn baby. "Give us a little smile!" is one of the first requests which the mother, or nurse, or some other adult makes to a baby, alarmed by its unwavering gravity—a request met, incidentally, by the baby's impassive disgust. The baby's expression remains serious; it knows that there is nothing to laugh at from the very beginning, that there is nothing funny in the antics of adults. Churchill has always left me with the singular impression of being this phenomenon, at once the alpha and omega of man, because of his precocious plumpness, his capacity for silence, a sort of brooding immersion in himself, his natural majesty.

After the fall of Tobruk, which caused him almost unbearable mental distress, the Desert Army rallied. The Prime Minister, back from America, hastened with Lord Ismay to the spot to inspect the men and their equipment. A twenty-four-hour automobile ride across the desert! Pug (Lord Ismay's nickname, like Churchill's inseparable companion, his famous dog), though much younger, was overwhelmed by fatigue. His head nodded; he was fast asleep. Churchill was chewing his cigar, his eyes riveted

33

on a map feebly illuminated by a dim light inside the car.

"Pug," said the Prime Minister gently, leaning over his sleeping companion. No answer. Then, grasping his arm and shaking him: "Pug, do you think you are in your basket?" Pug slept on, so he added in a louder voice: "Pug, are you dead?"

Churchill was a lonely child. As in the case of many children, throughout his childhood he was subject to vague presentiments, excesses of unsatisfied longing and periods of intense unhappiness. If we delve into the early history of celebrated men we find an explanation for most aspirations toward improved social conditions. Humble folk live in the shadow of the great; if we observe their children with sufficient care, we find that their childhood problems are the same. From the child's point of view, it matters little whether his mother goes out to work in a factory or out to a ball or the opera; in any case he is left alone. It is true that the working woman comes back home in the evening. Not so for Winston. Will there be nobody when he goes to bed, when it is dark, to lean over the cot in which he has been imprisoned for the night, to tuck in the future First Lord of the Admiralty, the future Prime Minister, to cuddle him, to take his mind off his fears with a story, to sing him a song, to give him a sense of security and the feeling of being loved exclusively by at least one person? Fortunately for Winston, his Nanny was there to sing to him and teach him the whole gamut of nursery rhymes—his guardian angel in starched collar and cuffs. All Nannies are God's gift to the lonely sons of our prominent men and their beautiful wives. The ladies who visited Winston, his relatives and his mother's friends, were daytime goddesses, even Aunt Leonie. They swept into the nursery in the afternoon, on holidays and birthdays, bringing with them the noises of the great world, their perfumed finery, their feather boas, their bouquets, and their flower-decked hats. They had come from afar and would soon be going away again, who knows where? They filled the little boy's heart with strange nostalgic longings which he could neither understand nor express. But when they had gone, these gift bringers and bearers of toys, the child was left alone, night fell and he was puzzled.

Luckily Nanny was there, to distract his mind from thoughts about the plurality of worlds. The cheerful sound of water running into his bath, her large and capable hands which clasped him so firmly . . . the layer of melancholy over his soul would soon be scrubbed away by the rich soapy lather, thanks to Nanny, who fed him, washed and dried him, kept him entertained, encouraged and forgave him. It was not only the hour for his bath, the delights of splashing and being dried with a soft bath towel, the hour for gruel and biscuits and the last sweet, but also the hour of the angel of prayer and the reassuring kiss, the friendly face close to his. "Good night, darling, God bless you!" to which he would answer, "God bless you, Nanny," every night for seven years. . . .

THE COURAGE TO DEFY HIS
SCHOOLMASTERS

IN APRIL 1888 there were few boarders in Mr. Davidson's house at Harrow—fourteen in all. They were not
particularly pleased to find their numbers increased by
the arrival of Spencer Churchill, whose Christian name
was Winston.

Nobody paid much attention to this redheaded new
boy, who only spent one year in Mr. Davidson's house.
One of the survivors among his contemporaries at that
time, Sir Gerald Woods Wollaston, freely admits this fact
in his study, "Churchill at Harrow." He admits also that the
spirit of prophecy was totally lacking both in the masters
and the boys. Nevertheless, the first day of his first term
should have been marked by some sign. His delivery was
defective and, strange to say, he stuttered in a manner
peculiar to himself. His speech was not indistinct—there
was no trace of harelip in the firmly drawn mouth—but
something seemed to make him chew and turn over every
word several times before allowing it to escape from his
lips. It was as if he wanted to suck all the juice out of it
and savor its taste to the full; a kind of satisfied grunt
accompanied this operation. Could this be considered a
fault in diction? Or was it the boy's way of attracting attention when he said something? It was difficult to decide.

He was not an easy boy to understand. One had to get used to him first.

Many years later, I was to think that my initial difficulty in hearing what he said was due to my imperfect knowledge of the English language, though I was most anxious not to miss any of his words, realizing that they were bound to be noteworthy. One gradually becomes accustomed to his peculiar delivery. It was already attracting attention; later, when he had become the inimitable orator the whole world admired, he was more often imitated by the current generation of students than any other man. It was considered a distinction to be able to give a good imitation of Churchill.

The only surviving fellow boarder assures us that no vestige remains of Winston's brief stay in Mr. Davidson's house, that his presence was almost completely ignored, and that when he moved to another house at Harrow, much larger, with a complement of sixty boys, nobody noticed his leaving, which caused no regrets. His departure was like his arrival—the general reaction was completely negative. Young prodigy as Winston already was, he left not the slightest mark on the imagination of the boys in Mr. Davidson's house nor, which is a serious reflection on that master, on Mr. Davidson himself.

A nobody, a little boy with carroty hair who talked as if he were chewing a caramel, had come and then gone, and not one of the fourteen paid the slightest attention. The headmaster alone, Dr. Weldon, made an exception in his case, admitting him to the school in spite of the established rules. Was it an intuition? Had he read the future in the boy's eyes, in his expression of pride and self-confidence? Did he suspect that the boy was a case of phenomenal obstinacy of purpose, which concealed an indomitable character worthy of encouragement for ends still wrapped in the mists of the future? Whatever his reasons, to the surprise of the other masters the headmaster decided to admit Spencer Churchill to Harrow School, in spite of the fact that he had completely failed in all subjects in the entrance examination.

After sitting for two hours in front of a page on which he was supposed to write a Latin translation, when he handed it in it was still completely blank. He had written nothing; not a line, not even a word. He had ruminated for two hours, incapable of translating his thoughts into action, and he had preferred to make no attempt to do a bad job. Dr. Weldon was severely criticized by the other masters for his decision; his partiality for the young Churchill was not attributed to any vision of the future, but simply to the headmaster's disinclination to reject the son of such a celebrated politician as Lord Randolph Churchill, on the assumption that this scion of the Marlborough family was bound sooner or later to make his way in the world in spite of the immediate prospect, which was highly discouraging. Churchill was to have the invidious distinction of being at the bottom of his class, persistently for a whole year, a fact hardly calculated to silence Dr. Weldon's critics.

Though he knew that he had been admitted as a special favor—others might call it an act of gross favoritism —this was not enough to spur on young Churchill to make the necessary effort to relinquish the humiliating position of the lowest in his class—he seemed resolutely determined to cling to it.

He soon found himself singularly unpopular because of his contempt for all the established rules of the school. The boys had no objection to the masters' laws being transgressed, but that their own traditional code should be neither respected nor obeyed by a new boy was intolerable and deserved the severest punishment.

Let us begin our sketch of young Churchill in his early days at Harrow by considering him in relation to his masters. What did they think of him? Satisfied, even priding himself on being at the bottom of the class, he seems to have convinced them that he completely lacked ambition. They were accustomed to the routine of competition in work and games, which enabled them to work the scholastic system satisfactorily. Its function was to supply England, generation after generation, with its necessary quota of leaders. Harrow prided itself on being able to turn out first-class scholars and exceptional men just as well as Eton; their methods are, for all practical purposes, identical. If it is true that the Battle of Waterloo was won on the playing fields of Eton, it is no less true of the playing fields of Harrow. But here was a boy altogether different from the others—neither competitive examinations nor competitive games under the open sky were sufficient stimulus to arouse, in that sluggish mind and body, the primordial British instinct of superiority. The masters were irritated by such an anomaly. Was his mother's

39

American blood responsible for it? It was difficult to be-lieve that the blood of the great Marlborough flowed through his veins.

At the end of Queen Victoria's reign a wind of new ideas was blowing against the old traditions, even in the great public schools, the preserves of the Old England. Everywhere new ideas were fermenting, and scathing denunciations of the Old Order could be heard even in-side the House of Commons. There a few voices were raised against the principle of the hereditary transmission of social status which it was argued was not matched by a similar transmission of character and ability. Was not what the agriculturists and stock breeders had found to be true also true of human beings? Allowed, fresh blood was sometimes introduced, but Winston Churchill was not as yet a successful example of this practice. Some Lib-eral had the effrontery to say to a crowded House of Com-mons that "their Lordships are like potatoes, the best part of them is under the ground!" Would young Churchill, descendant of the great Marlborough, continue this downward progress?

"It is very strange," said a witty Frenchwoman. *"Je me demande pourquoi les* grand-*pères n'ont jamais que de* petits-*fils."* The English vocabulary—the ideas suggested by the words—differs in many respects from the French vocabulary; one point in particular has always surprised and amused me; in English, grandfathers and grand-mothers are obliged to say "my grandson" or "my grand-daughter" when speaking of their children's offspring. Ab-solute equality has thus been established a priori between the first and the third generations. This obligatory use of the term great or grand has its advantages and disadvantages. As an Englishwoman, the old Duchess of Marlborough could not say, speaking of little Winston, anything but "my grandson"! During his school career, what use would young Churchill make of this hereditary greatness which, incidentally, facilitated his entry into Harrow? Nothing but to tear it in shreds—systematically, one would say, judging by his behavior.

For some reason which his masters, good humanists all, could not fathom, this boy seemed to have a real aversion to Latin; he could not or would not learn Cicero's language. Whenever there was a Latin class, he lost his tongue; he stumbled over the easiest words—those which had been passed on from Latin to French and from French to English at the Norman Conquest. He had no intention of knowing or learning anything which was not in current use. The classics were then the touchstone for distinguishing first-class brains. Greek and Latin were, so to speak, the time-tested filters which the schoolmaster used for clarifying that repulsive magma, the unformed mind of civilized man. Those whose function it was to educate him were disconcerted by his low showing of intelligence in the study of Latin. His masters became discouraged, made excuses and, naturally, became hostile to him. Young Churchill could not care less; he stayed in the fourth form for an indeterminate period. His name does not figure on the prize list at the end of the year. From the classical side he was sent to swell the ranks of the duffers on the modern side (which implied what his masters thought of his mental equipment). Even then as he persisted, quite shamelessly, in displaying his aptitude for learning nothing, not even modern idiom, the so-called living languages, he eventually gravitated into a class reserved for those who were, quite simply, being prepared for the army.

His career at Harrow is remarkable for two things: his obstinate refusal to learn anything which he did not find interesting (in other words, the audacity to claim the right to choose the subjects he was willing to assimilate); and, worse still, his claim to the right to choose the masters from whom he would consent to learn. This singular schoolboy had gone to school with the idea of educating himself as he pleased and when he pleased, choosing one subject rather than another entirely on his own, without asking anybody's advice. Such a procedure was unheard-of and disapproval was unanimous. Nevertheless, he profited by this self-selected, one-sided education, thanks to the help of the only master capable of encouraging his efforts to perfect himself in the one subject which interested him. This master was a Mr. Somerwell, and his subject was English. It was this remarkable man who was responsible for setting him on the educational path which would lead to his becoming Prime Minister. He was a man whom Churchill admired and liked, and the only master whose teaching methods he approved of. It was this man who put the weapon into his hands which allowed him to conquer. Churchill forges it, sharpens it, polishes it, and learns to use it in his own way, so that he will renew the genius of the language to which he is heir, in both its spoken and written forms.

As soon as Churchill feels that he is moving in the right direction he sticks to it with extraordinary perseverence. The schoolboy who defied his masters, refuted their arguments, refused to ape their way of thinking, avoided being poured into the usual mold, obstinately refused to learn classics, suddenly became passionately interested in the only language which he feels is necessary for the expression of his thoughts. He was yet to become the great expert in the use of English words, with an intimate understanding of their anatomy, their derivation, their essence, their rhythm, their functional significance, their power of suggestion, all that potential of forces accumulated throughout centuries by all the generations which hand the language on from one to another. From the moment he entered the political arena, his mastery of the English language was his highest and perhaps his only trump card; he has taken endless pains to acquire it and as it covers both the spoken and the written word, his sword is double-edged—a most unusual phenomenon, as a gifted writer is very rarely a gifted orator and *vice versa*.

Churchill was separated from Mr. Somerwell when he was moved from the classics class, in which he had learned nothing, to the modern language class, where he still learned none of them except in the most superficial way. Instead he concentrated on an exclusive study of the great poets, historians and prose writers who have

43

added to the glory of the English language; and later, when he was transferred to the class which catered to boys intending to go into the army, it was the English master alone, a Mr. Moriarty, who was able to make Churchill work. Winston was already a specialist; he acted exactly as if his future career entirely depended upon one thing—complete possession of the English language. This is in contradistinction to the overwhelming majority of men, who expect their years of schooling to give them a smattering of many subjects.

Throughout these years of lopsided schooling, during which the brilliant qualities of his mind were beginning to emerge, the only masters to be of any real help to him were these two and a third, a Mr. Mayo, who was his mathematics master in the army class. The latter appeared on his horizon almost too late; in six months Churchill made sufficient progress in mathematics to enable him to pass the entrance examination to Sandhurst.

His facility for expressing himself had its disadvantages. To put a final touch to his lamentable reputation with the masters, he was summoned by the headmaster to answer for a series of articles which had appeared in the *Harrovian,* a magazine published by the boys. According to tradition, none of the articles was signed. But Churchill's style then as now was unique and unmistakable. The headmaster said to him: "My boy, it has come to my knowledge that certain articles which have appeared recently in the *Harrovian* are of such a character as to be liable to undermine the respect of the boys for the duly constituted authorities of this establishment. In view of the fact that the *Harrovian* only publishes anonymous articles, I have not the slightest intention of setting an inquiry on foot to ascertain the authorship of this impertinent rubbish. But if any more articles of the same kind appear, I shall be reluctantly compelled to give you a good caning."

In these articles, his ideas had been so forcefully expressed and the masters had been so virulently criticized that the headmaster had been "reluctantly compelled" to conclude that they had been written by a born satirist who had never succeeded in translating or even reading Juvenal.

Outside the classroom, he was never at a loss for an answer. Parents and teachers alike usually insist upon children listening to their reprimands in silence and not answering back. To expect Churchill not to answer back proved to be an impossible proposition, first at Harrow and then later in the House of Commons. By now, there are so many legends about him that it is difficult to establish the authenticity of all the answers and extemporary repartees which are attributed to him. They are so numerous that it is to be expected that some are apocryphal; after all "it is only to the wealthy that money is lent"; and this epigram can be aptly applied to Churchill's witticisms. But now that he is on a pinnacle, he can afford to ignore such things as can his historiographers, who are the depositors of his oral tradition.

"Who was the author of that witticism of yours?" somebody asked Rivarol. "It must be my own, because it is extremely clever," was the answer. The repartee, the rapier-like reply, products of congenital insolence while he was still a schoolboy at Harrow, were early indications of his unpredictable character, of that combative ardor which, once aroused, was to persist up to the final victory. If the answer which the biographers of his early years have made a classic were not true, it would deserve to be remembered because it is so eminently probable. He was summoned to appear before the dread figure of his headmaster for having broken a rule of the school in a particularly flagrant manner: "Churchill," said the headmaster, "I have very serious reasons for being displeased with you." "And I, sir," answered Winston, "have other reasons, equally serious, to be displeased with you."

THE COURAGE TO DEFY HIS
SCHOOLMATES

STRANGE to relate, the fact that young Churchill was highly unpopular with his schoolmasters did not have the effect of making Lord Randolph Churchill's son popular with his schoolmates, and for cogent if not straightforward reasons. He had no *esprit de corps*; he disliked team games such as cricket and rugby, which are the soul of an English school. He specialized in sports of a subtler, strictly individualistic variety, very different from team games. When athletic distinctions were pinned up on the board, his name appeared as the winner of the fencing competition and was conspicuously lacking from any of the other lists. He handled a foil like a fencing master. One might almost think that he had done it on purpose, to win a bet. In fencing he chose the most un-English of all sports. As dueling has been illegal in England for more than a century, fencing has become rare and as a sport is now mainly regarded as continental rather than insular, since most of its distinguished exponents are either French or Italian, apart from students and others in Germany.

Churchill's only feat as a sportsman was to win the public school foils competition. True it was a sports distinction for his school, but in a form considered as the lowest rung of the competitive ladder. His schoolmates' grudging approval was lukewarm in character. His second but lesser achievement was in a sport which is also strictly individualistic—he won a prize for swimming. One is alone in swimming, as one is alone when on guard, lunging or striking, foil in hand.

Churchill did not distinguish himself in the Harrow School Officers' Training Corps. A humorous explanation for this has been given us by one of his schoolmates at the time. The O.T.C. at Harrow was affiliated to the Middlesex Regiment; the training consisted of drill in the quadrangle, followed at regular intervals by maneuvers in the surrounding country.

According to one of Wellington's famous remarks, military training is mainly concerned with exercises involving withdrawal or retreat. When the man who defeated Napoleon was asked what was the main factor which had contributed to his victories in Spain, and in particular Torres Vedras, he answered philosophically: "I commanded a corps of officers who were gentlemen, and who always knew the right moment to run away." There was already something in Churchill's character which reacted violently against any idea of "beating a retreat." Further, the drill for retreat made it necessary for the corporals, of whom Churchill was one, to carry the younger boys' rifles, so that they could run away more quickly. This was by no means the future officer's idea of fun. Besides, his martial instincts were to express themselves along entirely different lines.

His refusal to carry the rifle of one of the younger fugi-

tives added fuel to the fire of his great and persistent unpopularity among his schoolmates.

An incident to which Churchill himself has alluded in
his war memoirs, the principal hero of which was none
other than a boy called Leo Amery, who was Winston's
contemporary at Harrow, deserves mention, because the
conflict between these two Harrovians throws a revealing
light on both their characters. These two boys who fought
each other so strenuously were destined to become fellow
ministers in the same Cabinet; they were the successive
occupants of the office of First Lord of the Admiralty. One
day, catching sight of a little boy whom he took for a
fourth form boy like himself (which automatically entitled him to play a practical joke if he wanted to),
Churchill was ill-advised enough to trip the boy up and
send him head first, fully clothed, into the swimming pool.
The victim was Amery, an older boy in a higher form.
According to the unwritten law of the school, Churchill
had committed a crime. Amery climbed out of the swimming pool, hurled himself at his aggressor. Churchill, far
from apologizing, cried, "You are so small, I took you for
a boy of my own age!" But realizing at once that he had
touched a sore spot, with a kindliness which reveals the
streak of sentimentality in him but which he has always
been so skillful at concealing, he added, "My father, who
is a great man, is a very small man too!" Amery, tiny in
stature but endowed with great physical strength and a
school champion gymnast, was touched by this gesture
of boyish generosity and forgave his aggressor.

Nevertheless, his schoolmates could never bring themselves to condone his open contempt for all the rules and
for the unwritten law respected by everybody else and
which Churchill calmly transgressed with the quiet courage of somebody to whom other people's opinions seemed
nonexistent. The antipathy of his fellow Harrovians was
expressed in two often quoted examples: Churchill, in
direct violation of the rules, kept his dogs in a private
house in West Street; worse still, he openly took them for
walks in front of everybody, accompanied by a town boy
with whom he had made friends. Such a spectacle had
never been seen before and should never be seen again;
it was a simultaneous flaunting of his contempt for the
rules, and his love of dogs, a sentiment shared by most
of the boys but one which they were obliged to leave un-
expressed.

The second incident concerned an older boy called
Hicks—who became Bishop of Lincoln. He was then the
head prefect of the future Prime Minister's house and the
younger boy, Churchill, was the other boy's "fag," or
servant. Consequently Hicks' authority over him was
almost absolute; his orders were to be carried out to the
letter—brushing his boots or his clothes, or running er-
rands. It was one of Hicks' privileges to cane the boys
who had incurred his displeasure by slacking in carrying
out his fagging or being guilty of some offense against the
rules of the school. On the first occasion—often to be repeated in the future—on which Churchill rendered himself liable to punishment by Hicks, as soon as the caning
was over he turned around and said to Hicks, "I shall rise

above you later on!" To which Hicks replied without hesitation, "You shall have two more strokes for what you
have just said!" and he administered them. As he went
out, Churchill said to Hicks, "I am leaving, but what I
said, stands!"

THE COURAGE TO FACE RIDICULE

THE second, but more memorable, occasion on which Churchill the unsatisfactory schoolboy demonstrated his poor judgment and his kind heart has gone down in the annals of Harrow and will never be forgotten, thanks to one of his few surviving contemporaries, who has told the story with delicacy of feeling.

This incident did Churchill a great deal of harm at the time with his schoolmates. Now that time has done its work, it will be regarded today as an example of one of his most lovable forms of courage, at a period when his physical and mental well-being depended on what the boys with whom he was obliged to live at Harrow thought of him. Little Winston, as we have related, tenderly loved the Nanny who had brought him up. With brazen effrontery Churchill, one holiday, dared something which no one had dared to do before him—he invited his old Nanny to come and see him at school. He took her over the buildings, to the delight of the poor woman who felt unspeakably happy and realized what honor was being paid to her.

Not content with showing her the classrooms, the dining hall, his own room, the chapel, the quadrangle and the various outbuildings, at the risk of being seen in his Nanny's company by the masters and, worse still, by the boys engaged in their usual games, he went further:

52

chivalrously offering her his arm, he dared to walk up and down High Street of Harrow with his Nanny so that everybody could see him with her, and then he saw her off at the station. She left, in a daze of grateful happiness, proudly conscious of the fact that the boy whom she had brought up with such loving care was an exception to the cruel rule which obliges boys, when they are about to become men, to feel ashamed of their first warmhearted affections.

It is difficult to overestimate the degree of courage displayed by Churchill when he faced the storm of ridicule with which all the boys, without exception, overwhelmed him on this occasion; we are given some idea by his contemporary and biographer who does not hesitate to write: "This unprecedented action of Churchill's (proof of his indifference to the opinion of others when his affections were involved) will always be remembered to his credit, though at the time it considerably increased the dislike and contempt of his school-fellows."

"More than one of us," adds Sir Gerald Woods Wollaston, "felt the same sentiments of gratitude towards some old Nanny, which we would have liked to express in the same way. But no one else would have had the courage."

At the time, the news that Churchill had been seen in public with his Nanny spread like wildfire throughout the whole school. The boys sneered at him and pulled his leg publicly; he was generally looked down on, taunted, insulted, smothered in sarcasm long after the event. The strong turned away from him, disgusted by this abject proof of childish sentimentality, hence weakness; the weak did not dare make any sign of approval. "As for me," adds the biographer of those dim and distant days at Harrow, "I have vainly regretted, a thousand times regretted, right up to the present time, that I was too cowardly, when at the school, to give my old Nanny the satisfaction of being seen on my arm, walking up the High Street in full view of everybody; only Churchill was bold enough, had enough courage to face ridicule" (from "Churchill at Harrow").

Churchill, unlike most Englishmen, admits frankly that he hated those years spent at school and that he could think of nothing that he would loathe more than to have to live them over again. The usual attitude is quite the contrary and, here again, he shows himself the born nonconformer by going against the generally expressed opinion that those years are a man's best years and that it would be bliss if it were possible to go back to them. Winston denies it and proves it—contrary to the habits of many, who expatiate endlessly on their happy times at public school and pay their old school periodic visits in order to revive what they have agreed to call "the best memories of the happiest time of their lives."

Churchill left Harrow at Christmas, in 1892; he revisited his old school on one single occasion, in October 1900, to give a lecture about the South African War and his experiences as correspondent of the *Morning Post*, when he was taken prisoner by the Boers and succeeded in escaping.

Forty years were to pass before he paid his second visit.

This time he returned to Harrow as Prime Minister, when war was raging, accompanied by his wife and some of the members of his government. On that occasion he spoke to the boys (and probably also to Hicks' ghost). The enthusiasm of the boys who surrounded the man on whom the safety of England and the free world then depended, was unbounded. After applauding frantically, they broke into the famous Harrow school song which old and young, the Prime Minister at their head, intoned:

> So, today—and Oh, if ever
> Duty's voice is ringing clear
> Bidding men to brave endeavour,
> Be our answer, "We are here."

Since then, each year, Churchill has returned to his old school, to join the young boys in singing the song dear to all Harrovians. In one speech, he said to them: "Our public school system is a good one because these institutions help to form character, continuing invariably throughout the centuries to give to the nation new generations of young people who have learned by service to lead."

But as he possesses, as well as so many other forms of courage, the courage of sincerity, he has also said to them: "Has life no greater joys to offer you than your years at school? That has not been my own experience. . . ."

If he revisits his old school, as he has now revisited it annually for nearly thirteen years, it is not for the purpose of telling the boys that he was happy there. He frankly added on the occasion of his last visit: "I am of the opinion that the public school system should be maintained," but he confessed to his listeners that he had no desire to wear out his trousers again on the school benches nor to resume his old place—that of the lowest boy in his form.

THE COURAGE TO PLAY THE DUNCE

NOT everyone has the gift to be a dunce. Those who boast about it and are dunces because they cannot help it would be ill-advised to base their argument on young Churchill's experiences, in an attempt to make their masters or their family believe that they are heaven-sent geniuses and thus explain their inability to learn anything or to pass any examination.

In Churchill's case, the decision to learn only what is most useful to him, both in the present and the future, stemmed, in the schoolboy, then the student, then the cadet, from a prophetic sense of his destiny. He knew the time and place, and divined the adverse circumstances in which all his faculties would have to come into play, develop, overcome all obstacles, and prevail, according to his own laws and the rhythm of his character. It is as if there were a hidden fire within, which gives him the propulsive power necessary for hurtling forward to meet each event in his life. He rejects everything which can retard him. The unconstrained ease with which he rids himself of superfluous weights is such that after having failed to satisfy his masters, disappointed his family, astounded his schoolmates, he has no choice but to proclaim himself a dunce and consider himself one. But this is to last only until the indisputable proof has been forthcoming that he has his own method, entirely created by himself, for

solving major problems—a method which, in the end, he
will be able to vindicate. In rejecting a classical education,
he was able to persuade at least two of his masters, one
after the other, to forgive and understand him; they will
help him in turn to forge the only weapon which he will
need for the supreme fight, which will be his whole life:
his style. He has attained complete mastery of the English
language, as it is spoken and written. He will leave school
adequately equipped to grapple with his fate. There is
nothing to prove that a brain like his has not been inherited by virtue of a sort of vaccine (by a phenomenon
of osmosis which is still very obscure, but in which I have
my own reasons for believing), contributed to by a long
line of ancestors, all educated to become leaders by this
classical humanism in which the ruling classes of England
have been steeped, generation after generation. Pericles'
discourse to the Athenians, he will live it! So, why bother
to learn it? Had his father and his grandfather and the
latter's great grandfather not been Latin scholars? Was
he not already conscious of the fact that he needed the
blank page, on which he was supposed to write his first
Latin translation, for inscribing those thoughts of his,
those words, which will become powerful engines to raise
the British people, higher than its own standards, to the
summits of sacrifice?

Having left Harrow without honors, with barely enough
credits to be admitted to Sandhurst, Churchill will put
his future biographers in the difficulty of trying to find an
anecdote which will give form and color to his decision to become a soldier, a course which was originally

thought of by his masters as a last resort. For lack of anything better, his historians will use the old saw about the
little boy playing with tin soldiers. Churchill himself is
said to have been responsible for it. Where there is an
end, there must be a beginning, a theme is the soul of a
symphony, like the distribution of color tones in a painting. No one realizes this better than Churchill himself,
who is also, above all, a composer, an artist, the greatest
stage producer in the world. He felt compelled to make
his chroniclers a present of this trite image of childhood,
so suitable for appealing to the popular imagination—the
little boy, lining up his Lilliputian combatants for battle
under the eye of his amused father, Lord Randolph. The
future commander-in-chief, on all fours on the carpet
where the decisive battle is being fought, Winston in
knickers, is asked by the author of his days: "Do you want
to be a soldier?" The immediate answer is in the affirma-
tive; of course, without a shadow of hesitation, he wants
to be a soldier and become commander-in-chief. The anecdote no doubt pleased his advisers at the time when a
decision as to a career for this inveterate dunce had to be
made. To enter Sandhurst a special, in fact an extra-
special, course of studies was essential! Though an object
has been found for the ambition of Winston Churchill,
the road will be long and tedious.

"Everything and everything at once," seems to be his
motto. At this period of his life he wanted everything and
was simmering with impatience for it, he had to call on all
his reserves of courage; once more he had to lean his el-
bows on a table and open his bulky textbooks. More im-

portant, he called on the good offices of Captain James. This gentleman was the proprietor of an establishment which at that time catered to all the backward boys who wanted to be admitted to Sandhurst. It was commonly called "Jimmy's" and was a haven for all the budding corps commanders and future field-marshals who wanted to learn something about military subjects—the art of making war according to the principles established as far back as the times of Cyrus and Alexander. Captain James was the first and most famous of those crammers on whom families rely for exorcizing their dunces.

Churchill took along with him to Jimmy's a head which did not take kindly to stuffing or cramming. It is a far cry from the little boy playing with his tin soldiers at the foot of his great ancestor's statue, even if the blood in his veins is that of the victor of Blenheim. It is a long way from this child to the cadet, capable of assimilating everything that has to be learned in order to win a modern war. Wars will never be as modern as I am, thought young Churchill. But was there anybody to whom he could say it aloud? Captain James would laugh at him. So he had to demean himself and join the ranks, suffer himself to be led and, above all, let Jimmy have his way. Jimmy was the great expert in cramming, full of experience and knowledge, who had filled generations of empty heads. With what? With obsolete teachings, traditional methods, meaningless rules-of-thumb, thought Churchill. He knew that they would be useless the next day, in view of the rapid development of modern life, with its increasingly unexpected twists and turns. In his opinion, military education (if it is to be of any real value) must take change into account and modify itself as quickly as events demand, even more so, if possible.

Once inside Captain James's "forcing-house," Churchill did his best to co-operate and allow himself to be crammed with the facts for which he had no use. Nevertheless he was very careful not to overload his memory nor let them clip the wings of his imagination. When he wants to, he can remember anything; in fact, his memory is phenomenal. When he was still at Harrow, and at the bottom of his form to boot, he dumbfounded everybody and won a school prize—without, alas, affecting his marks at the end of term examination—by reciting twelve hundred lines of Macaulay's "Lays of Ancient Rome," without stopping to take a breath and without a single mistake. He also knows whole scenes of Shakespeare's plays by heart, and has never hesitated to stop and correct his masters if they misquote; another manifestation of this aristocratic faculty of "taking pleasure in displeasing," which has been largely responsible for his unpopularity and remained with him even in Captain James's establishment.

This strange dunce carefully hoarded his prodigious memory and barred the door into his Palace of Mnemosyne to all knowledge, all teaching which seemed to him insipid or superfluous. Needless to say this causes him to be singled out in an even more invidious manner. The student who tries his best and fails, is to be pitied; but the one who is able to succeed and does not try is an abomination to his teachers. In spite of his reputation as

61

an infallibly successful crammer throughout his long career, the head of Jimmy's was ready to give up hope of being able to accomplish this too manifestly thankless task: to make sure that the young Churchill's standard was high enough to pass the Sandhurst entrance examination. He failed twice; at the third try, when he finally passed, his marks were too low for him to be admitted to anything but a cadetship that qualified him to become a cavalry officer, a branch of the service which involved very little book work and gave plenty of scope for the most exuberant imagination.

The charge of the Light Brigade at Balaclava was still fresh in many people's memory; it belonged to the romantic tradition to which, at the end of the Victorian era, the young men destined to be soldiers still clung with enthusiasm. The romance of nineteenth-century England was to end in a last cavalry charge, in which Churchill would take part; in history it is called the charge of Omdurman.

Part Two

THE COURAGE TO CHARGE

WINSTON CHURCHILL, born in the Blenheim Palace, amidst trophies and panoplies, surrounded by paintings depicting battle scenes and tapestries of warlike subjects, came to the conclusion, while still a small boy, that cavalry charges lead to glory and wealth. It is legitimate to assume that he considered the courage to charge the most enviable form of heroism, to attain which a man of noble lineage should strive with all his might. "Man is the animal made for glory," said Tertullian; the axiom was to be borne out by the budding cavalry officer, young Churchill on the threshold of Sandhurst.

After twelve years of schooling, the unhappiest years of his life left behind without regret, he could now proceed to do something for which he believed he was supremely fitted by nature. One of Marcel Proust's passages describing the death of Robert de Saint-Loup (modeled by Proust on Bertrand de Fénélon who died for France in 1916) seems to me singularly appropriate for describing "gentleman-cadet" Churchill's state of mind at that time: "He must have been a magnificent sight, in those last hours; in life, he had always seemed poised for a charge, even when sitting down or walking across a drawing-room, his smile being calculated to dissimulate the indomitable will-power contained in that triangular head; at last he had charged; the books now cleared away, the feudal tower had been restored to its original military function."

It was at Sandhurst that young Churchill prepared himself for the charge. By doing what? By reading a multitude of historical studies and works on the art of making war—ancient, less ancient, right down to the most modern. Throughout his life he was to continue reading and studying and being fascinated by them. Among them was a classic by the great Marlborough, his ancestor. And then, in view of the fact that the horse, that "ambulating throne," as the poet Paul Claudel describes it, is a seat for which he had a passion, he spent much time training himself in horsemanship, proficiency in which requires not only a natural gift but patient and unremitting practice. He believed that a rider could not take too much trouble to win the confidence and co-operation of his horse. He considered his riding lesson the most enjoyable part of his day; he threw himself body and soul into equestrian exercises which were part of the curriculum, both inside and outside the riding school, and soon he acquired a wonderful mastery of the art of riding. In December 1894 he had finished his training and left Sandhurst, having placed eighth in his class of one hundred and fifty cadets. He was gazetted second-lieutenant in the Fourth Hussars, then stationed at Aldershot.

There, in what is called the Long Valley, he proved himself a fine horseman in the fullest sense of the word; he applied himself sedulously to the training given to cavalry officers of the British Army. In the last years of the nineteenth century this consisted of long, exciting gallops, obstacle jumping, lance or drawn sword in hand, according to the tradition of the old, chivalrous England, in which all forms of riding were almost a national obsession. Polo was then one of the games which were regarded as a complement to military training proper; Churchill played it with characteristic gusto and enthusiasm and so often that it proved a great strain on his budget. During this period all he thought of was hand-to-hand fighting and charging (at least once in his life) at the head of a squadron, or better still, at the head of his own regiment, the Queen's Own Hussars. His Queen was the old Victoria, surfeited with glory, sinking beneath the weight of honors and her years, the crown of England on her head, the mantle of Empress of India on her octogenarian shoulders. For her Jubilee there was a flourish of trumpets on five continents from one end of the Empire to the other, but a horrible thought insinuated itself into the hussar second-lieutenant's mind: Was a cavalry charge still possible or even conceivable? Where and when? In what part of that Old World, now seeming to be suffering from a hardening of its arteries? At the tail-end of this nineteenth century (which at its beginning saw the death of Napoleon) any idea of further military glory seemed to be fated to dissolve into thin air. By then, the sun never set on the British Empire.

The morning gallops over the dew-covered grass of the Long Valley, jumping hedges, gates, hurdles, and streams gave him a carefree exhilaration. But how much longer

65

would he be able to wear his full-dress uniform, whose facings had a magnificent funereal significance, marking the ribs of the death's-head cavaliers; with the aigrettes on the shakos, and the saddles embroidered with the royal crest? Was this military pomp and warlike display not destined to disappear now that the name of a certain Mr. Maxim was appearing in the secret reports, as the inventor of a machine gun so light that it could be stuck into the ground or carried, for all practical purposes, as easily as a shooting-stick?

Nevertheless, Churchill's hopes were not to be dashed to the ground; he had visualized himself charging with the cavalry, just as in the battle paintings at Blenheim; it is inconceivable to this cavalryman that the war to come would deprive him of his horse, and of his dreams. . . .

His destiny is of such a kind as to leave the dreamer no respite. Reality must be manipulated to conform to imagination. Churchill sailed from England for Cuba in November 1895; he was accompanied by a friend, a young cavalry officer like himself, Reginald Barnes. One might wonder why they should embark at the beginning of the hunting season, when "those five glorious months of winter" are back at last, when the pink-coated hunt will gallop through the countryside behind hounds, after the fox. It is then that England becomes a paradise for the sportsmen who are keen on both hunting and riding. There must have been some very powerful attraction to make these young officers leave England's shores precisely at this season, to miss the delights of hunting which for centuries past had inspired the best artists to paint their best pictures, the engravers and even the caricaturists to produce a multitude of colored prints and drawings showing all stages of this most exciting pursuit of the slyest of animals. A love of nature and hunting are deeply ingrained in the life of England. Winston Churchill is a born huntsman. Obstacles have always stimulated him. What is the attraction which lured him away from home at the opening of the season so impatiently awaited by all the young officers of his regiment?

It was simply that he could not afford it, a situation which would often preoccupy him, take him off his course and juggle with his destiny, through the early part of his life. As he had spent every penny he possessed on buying polo ponies, there was nothing left to defray the expenses of a hunting season in England. With that faculty of summing up a situation at a glance and adopting the best alternative (in which he is to excel throughout his life), Churchill did one of his quick-change acts and gambled on a new card. Up to now he had tried every form of this combination except one; the risk of breaking his neck and the excitement of the chase are combined on the hunting field, but his lack of funds made it impossible for him to take part in the hunting season. Why not try the one form as yet denied him? Sport and war have been associated from the dawn of history. Churchill has always read the newspapers attentively, a habit he contracted soon after he learned to read. Besides, he was the grandson of Leonard Jerome, American journalist, and journalism in its most active form, reporting, had no secrets for him. He lost no time in discovering the one place in which something was stirring in the winter of 1895-6.

Though it is true that money never ensures either happiness or glory, as is epitomized by the moralist's dictum —*When we see the manner in which providence distributes the riches of this world, we understand why God attaches so little importance to money*—nevertheless, the delectable taste for inherited luxury to which Churchill's birth had accustomed him offered a thousand different forms of temptation to which young English aristocrats were particularly susceptible. It is a powerful incentive to younger sons to exert themselves as long as the biblical law of inheritance, making the eldest son the heir, remains in force.

Instinct rather than reason was the driving force behind Churchill's urge to be on the spot as quickly as possible, anywhere in the world where there was fighting or some upheaval, to risk his life, providing that he could write it up for his paper. Danger is one of the elements, perhaps the only one for a man of his kind, which makes life tolerable. The problem was how to contrive an invitation to go to Cuba? He knew that there was desperate fighting between the Spaniards and the guerilla bands supported by the United States of America, and that it could not continue indefinitely. Getting a permit for a sea passage was the problem.

No one could have hesitated less than Churchill to take advantage of his position as a member of a powerful family. He remembered that his father had been a friend of

Sir Henry Wolff, British Ambassador to Madrid. Without delay Churchill wrote to Sir Henry and asked him to approach the Spanish military authorities; he wanted permission to follow the campaign with the Spanish corps which was defending the island both against guerilla troops and against the policy at Washington, which was to take Cuba under cover of a smokescreen of anticolonial propaganda. The Minister of War at Madrid proved amenable—in fact, most obliging—and permission was granted to the young Churchill and his companion. They could go to Cuba, have their fill of fighting and show themselves to be good *caballeros*. Churchill's natural gifts as a storyteller combined with his uncanny evocative power—his descriptive style is magnificently colorful and picturesque—would no longer be limited to his private letters. By now the Cuban campaign had been dragging along for some time and barely impinged on the British public until its interest was captured by a series of articles written in a new and striking style which appeared in the *Daily Telegraph*.

When he reached Cuba, Churchill found the regular Spanish forces attempting to grapple with guerilla warfare—that underhand form of warfare which he was to have plenty of opportunity of observing on future occasions during his long life, in South Africa, in Ireland, Malaya, Indochina, and Kenya. The Spaniards fought with their traditional courage but used the old-fashioned methods which they had learned while acquiring their immense empire. The great island of Cuba was the last vestige of that empire and they were defending it with

69

blind heroism. Churchill witnessed feats of arms worthy of the great Cid, but they were wasted. Spanish troops proved helpless against the guerillas who attacked and melted into the bush; they were ambushed, betrayed, trapped, and decimated by every artifice contrary to the rules of open warfare. Churchill survived unscathed these skirmishes with an unseen enemy, but soon the government in Madrid came to the wise decision that the game was not worth the candle. Nothing was to be gained by spilling precious Spanish blood in a hopeless guerilla war.

Churchill's first bellicose adventure came to a sudden end. There is an element of chivalry in his espousal of the cause of Spain, foredoomed to be a lost cause. The one thing that Churchill brought back from Cuba (apart from the honor of having conducted himself like Don Quixote) was the habit of taking a siesta—a habit that was to serve him in good stead throughout his life. Sir Edward Marsh, Churchill's secretary and faithful friend, and his old traveling companion, has confessed to me that his old chief's example had taught him to make a point of a full hour's complete rest after lunch.

Churchill has steadfastly adhered to this habit contracted in Cuba and it is partly responsible for his superabundant vitality and astonishing capacity for work.

In this same year 1896, Churchill's eagerness and impatience to test his courage on the field of battle was given a further opportunity. His regiment, the 4th Hussars, left for India, where the northwest frontier was in a seriously disturbed state. At this period Churchill was consumed with two overriding ambitions: first and foremost to fight for his country; secondly to play and win for his regiment the interregimental polo challenge cup, competed for by teams representing the different cavalry regiments of the British Empire. The second of these was, perhaps, the more difficult of the two ambitions to fulfill. But both of them were to be triumphantly satisfied—thanks to his indefatigable audacity, and the courage never to be deflected from his objective once the objective had been clearly defined in his mind.

The 16th of September 1897 was a red-letter day for him. On that remarkable day British and Indian forces were attacked in the valley of the Mamunds.

The Mamunds, one of those tribes whose rebellious spirit was only equaled by their ferocity in battle, attacked General Sir Bindon Blood's brigade. It was a murderous engagement; the British brigade, too thinly deployed, lost a large number of men, British as well as Indian, and almost all the British officers were killed. Young Churchill, always prompt to hurl himself into the heart of the fray, determined to take full advantage of the opportunity, and continued the fight with the 31st Punjabis, an Indian regiment to which he had himself temporarily attached. His men performed prodigies of valor and it was thanks to them that the situation was saved.

Churchill must have had this occasion in mind forty-four years later when, as Prime Minister, he praised the Indian troops and personally decorated the men of this

71

regiment for their admirable conduct in the battle of Keren in Abyssinia. This was one of his full circles, one of those themes which recur in the great symphony and which largely account for the fact that his life is a masterpiece.

However, this was no time to harangue the troops drawn up on parade, and in any case Churchill was now recalled to his own regiment. With great reluctance he returned to his quarters in Bangalore to find that his colonel considered, not without reason, that it was high time for young Churchill to settle down. He must conform to the rules and accept the obligations of service with the 4th Hussars. But he still itched to be on the northwest frontier, where he believed the battle would continue and develop into a major campaign.

At Bangalore Churchill neglected no means in his power, including intrigues, flagrant violations of the Army code (even what might seem to the conventional mind as something which might remotely resemble desertion) to get back to the fighting on which he had set his mind. In his case, this was more than a virtue; it was a need, almost an obsession. In this situation he appealed to everybody, used all his influential connections, and he even went so far as to grant himself leave to which he was not entitled. To begin with, he asked his colonel to give him a few days off. The request granted, he rushed to general headquarters at Calcutta where he obtained an interview. The outcome of this was precisely nothing but he was by no means discouraged. At the same time he bombarded his mother with letters and telegrams—he knew that Lady Randolph Churchill was in London—begging her to intercede with her numerous friends on his behalf. Lady Randolph knew all the politicians worth knowing, both those who were in power and those who might be any moment. But everything failed, his plea to his commanding officer and all his vigorous wire-pulling. The desperately coveted prize of transfer to the frontier seemed to be escaping from his fingers.

At this point he decided once again to take matters into his own hands; he had no intention of being thwarted. He decided to appeal in person to the Commander-in-Chief of the Army in India, Sir William Lockhart. He told him everything, no doubt encouraged by the thought that if he did not succeed in arousing Sir William's sympathy, he would have to return to Bangalore and face his punishment for being absent without leave. The old warrior allowed himself to be persuaded. He even went so far as to appoint Churchill his own assistant orderly officer, a subterfuge by which Churchill would have been able to go back and join the troops who were fighting on the frontier. Fortune may favor the brave, but this time it was too late; dispatches had just arrived announcing that the tribes had submitted. The war was over!

What matter, another war was breaking out not very far away—in the Sudan. Without losing a moment, Churchill volunteered to carry the good news from India to London. Actually, his real purpose was to go to London to arrange for his own transfer; at all costs, he was determined to be sent to the Sudan. This time the difficulties were even more formidable than they were in India.

The recently appointed commander-in-chief, Sir Herbert Kitchener (later Lord Kitchener of Khartoum) was, it seems, firmly determined that Churchill should not be allowed to join the force under his command. Even when Churchill persuaded Lord Salisbury, the Prime Minister, to intercede in his favor with the commander-in-chief, Kitchener refused to allow himself to be persuaded or bullied into agreeing. At this point, either chance or Churchill's guardian angel took a hand. Inquiries disclosed to Churchill that Sir Evelyn Wood, Quartermaster-General of the Army in the Sudan, objected to Kitchener interfering with his province by appointing the officers himself, at that time usually a jealously guarded prerogative of the quartermaster. Realizing that his one chance of succeeding depended on exploiting this difference between his chiefs, Churchill made a direct appeal to Sir Evelyn Wood and persuaded him to override Kitchener's decision. As a result he was ordered to the 21st Lancers and to the Sudan.

On the eve of the Battle of Omdurman, Churchill appeared before Kitchener for the first time. The two men were destined to meet in wartime more than once, and to sit at the same table, in the council chamber at Downing Street. Churchill rode up to Kitchener to make a reconnaissance report from his regiment. He watched Kitchener ride forward, a superb horseman, imposing and rigid at the head of his army. Churchill had to make his brief report to Kitchener personally. They were face to face but the interview was a brief one; Churchill reported that the army of the Dervishes was advancing toward Omdurman, and a clash was inevitable.

The following day, the battle which smashed the power of the Dervishes and made Kitchener the master of the Sudan was joined. The 21st Lancers led the famous charge. Churchill was second-in-command at the extreme right of the line. In a few minutes, the 21st Lancers lost five officers, sixty-five men and a hundred and twenty horses. The army of the Dervishes was in headlong flight after losing what remained of the prestige of the last defenders of the Caliphate.

In November 1898, after Churchill's dream had come true, he rejoined his own regiment, the 4th Hussars, stationed in India. There, once again, he examined his financial position and found that the game of polo, in the style played by cavalry officers at that time, was entirely beyond his means. It was then that he decided to leave the army and earn his living by journalism, with the ultimate objective of going into Parliament. But before sending in his resignation, he was determined to carry out his second main ambition (which had been in his mind ever since he had been in India)—to win the inter-regimental polo competition, playing with the 4th Hussars' team. It was to be played in February at Meerut, 1,400 miles to the north of Bangalore. Never before had a regiment stationed in the south of India won the event. What had not been done before him, should be done by him. There was no doubt about it in his own mind. But the day before the match he was the victim of a disastrous mishap, which would probably have discouraged any other player. He dislocated his shoulder. He made light of the accident. He had his right elbow tightly bound to his body with stirrup-leather. Then, he galloped on to the field at the head of his team; he was number one. His function was to tackle the redoubtable Captain Hardress Lloyd, number one of the 4th Dragoon Guards' team. Throughout the game, Churchill attacked, harassed and crowded Lloyd without mercy. In the deciding chukker the 4th Hussars were leading 4 to 3, and Churchill, in spite of one arm being out of action, managed to score three out of the four goals. The victory of his team was his personal victory.

Churchill left India, the 4th Hussars, and the army in a blaze of glory.

THE COURAGE TO ENTER THROUGH
THE BACK DOOR

WHAT is most to be admired in this prodigious character in the process of formation? Is it a taste for dangerous adventures, or physical courage pure and simple? Both of these are the natural prerogatives of young men; there is nothing unusual about them. But what is exceptional in Churchill is his capacity for ringing the changes on the whole gamut of different forms of courage, for attempting every form of endurance in turn, as if to train his faculties as the athlete develops his muscles.

Among all the others, the courage to humiliate himself is one of the most praiseworthy. In giving up an honorable profession, after succeeding in making a name for himself (in spite of the handicap of having a name already celebrated in that profession), he could not avoid belittling himself in the eyes of his own social world. This young man's conduct must have astounded the pontiffs of the War Office, the chiefs of that professional army whose officers were gentlemen by definition. What—he flouts etiquette, he abandons the club, the company of his own class, which had to close its ranks in order to find a place for him, which shared his code of values and was able to appreciate his courage! After the aurora borealis of a promising career, how could they understand this young man who renounced everything that life held in store for him in the way of success and honors, at a single stroke of the pen, in a letter of resignation to the War Office?

In spite of them, in spite of the opposition of his own family, in spite of himself perhaps, he resigned all the same. He had decided to leave the army and that was that. The only aspect of the profession of soldiering which appealed to him was active campaigning; he disliked garrison life, club life and, above all, the daily humdrum routine. But as the two Indian frontier tribes had submitted, as Kitchener was at Khartoum, good-by. Once his resignation had been handed in, he would not be able to retract it; in any case he would not be willing to go back on his word. He will fight in another way, but he will never give up fighting.

In October 1899, Paul Krüger sent his ultimatum from Pretoria to the British Government; three days later, it was war. An enormous wave of unpopularity swept from the continent and broke over England. European public opinion was solidly against Great Britain, against its government, and even against its patriarchal old Queen. As a child, I heard the crowd in the streets of Paris shouting "Hurrah for Krüger!" I saw the old man who was selling, at the corner of the Avenue Marigny and the Champs Elysées, a special number of the *Rire* in which the poor grandmother of Europe, "Grandmama Queen," was represented with her skirts raised in the classical position, about to be given a spanking. The vender was extolling his merchandise in a hoarse voice which I can still vividly recall, "Who wants to see the —— of old Victoria? It will cost you two sous to see it!" Paris was in a ferment; Paris was also laughing; but at The Hague it was a more serious matter; the Germany of William II was prematurely exulting in the defeat of England and was openly proclaiming its hopes that this would be the end of that irksome little island. Even in America, influenced by Theodore Roosevelt, who was of Dutch extraction, they were abusing Albion.

A few days later, October 11th of that same year, young Churchill sailed for South Africa in the capacity of war correspondent for the *Morning Post*. What a disgrace, what a humiliation! said the old men in the clubs of London. The son of Lord Randolph had left the army to take up journalism! That despised calling, instead of the profession which would have given him the opportunity of fulfilling all his ambitions! All of them? Only Churchill knew how many they were. But what a disappointment for those who saw him go! Marlborough was going to war through the back door! Churchill had exchanged his arms for the reporter's pencil. He would write his communiqués in a journalist's notebook—what a scandal! He was the butt of ridicule as well. It was known in London military circles that a new rule had been established by the War Office, denying the status of combatant, the honorable qualification of soldier, to those who were so ill-advised as to comment on military operations in the pay of the London newspapers. This measure was largely due to young Churchill himself, who had taken the liberty of fighting and writing for the papers at the same time; a dual role which they considered intolerable and which had given his chiefs an excuse for promulgating the law of legitimate defense and protecting the army against the journalists.

His letters to the *Morning Post* and his book *The River War,* written during the war in the Sudan, followed letters sent periodically to the *Daily Telegraph,* signed *From a Young Officer,* a transparent anonymity in view of the fact that his style was already unmistakable and obviously recognizable to anybody who had ever received a letter from him. His mother had become his literary agent. It was she who had arranged for the publication of his articles by Longmans in book form under the title *History of a Company in the 1897 Malakand Campaign.* A photograph appeared on the cover of the book: a pensive young man with a prematurely bald forehead, who looked anything but the soldier exulting in battle, as described in the book.

Both the book and the portrait had an excellent press in London. The Prince of Wales, later King Edward VII, wrote a personal letter to the young author saying that he had read the book "with the greatest interest . . . only heard it spoken of with praise . . ."

The critic of the magazine *The Pioneer* declared that the author of this book manifested a degree of wisdom and understanding far beyond what was to be expected of a man of his age. Further, Churchill had discovered, on making out his balance sheet, that this little book, written in the course of a campaign, had in two months earned a net profit for him equivalent to two years' pay as a cavalry officer. This fact was largely responsible for his decision to leave the army.

The contempt with which the renegade lieutenant of the 4th Hussars, now the journalist Churchill, was regarded when he came on board the *Dunotter Castle* can easily be imagined; the ship was filled with officers, many of them of the General Staff, bound for South Africa under the orders of the commander of the single army corps, which was considered sufficient to make the Boers listen to reason. Sir Redvers Buller, the general commanding the expeditionary corps, though he tolerated the presence of Churchill on board the "military transport" fully endorsed the official War Office attitude toward this unusual war correspondent, now an amateur soldier and a professional journalist. He should be looked upon with the gravest suspicion by responsible commanders in the field. The double role of officer and war correspondent which Churchill had played during the fighting on the northwest frontier of India and then in the Sudan had now been rendered impossible and strictly forbidden. This prohibition applied to everybody and particularly to Churchill, who was directly responsible for the measure in question. Now there he was on his way to take part in the campaign, with the troops who were going to do the fighting, but considered by the General Staff as one of those "damned civilians" who describe operations from a distance and must be kept away from everybody even remotely responsible for the conduct of the war; in fact, he was going to enter South Africa with the armed forces of Her Britannic Majesty, but he would do so by the back door.

If he felt humiliated or offended, he took good care to make sure that no one knew it; he was answerable to himself alone, which made all the difference. A man is inferior only if he conceives himself to be so in a given situation, in which he has placed himself by his poor opinion of himself and which will persist as long as that opinion is maintained. We need fear nothing of the sort in young Churchill's case. Wherever he is, whatever he does, whatever other people may think of him, he is inspired by a burning conviction of being himself, always superior. What was really behind this change of profession? Simply this: he was experimenting on himself, trying out the different forms of courage which he will need to reach the appointed meeting place with his destiny, always a little farther on. The fact that, during the South African campaign, he rode into Johannesburg on his bicycle, quite alone, while this city was still in enemy hands, at the risk of being shot if captured, and succeeded in riding right through the city, seeing everything, like a one-man Trojan horse, forced the great chiefs to realize that this "war correspondent" corresponds to the ideal of a scout on a reconnoitering expedition rather than anything else.

Above all, he was now free to criticize the conduct of the war in South Africa. There was much to find fault with and he did not scruple to say so. His "daimone," to use Socrates' expression, inspired his diatribes against the inexcusable hesitations and delays in carrying out the war plan, which rendered it nugatory. The dilatory manner in which the operations designed to liberate Ladysmith were carried out was inconceivable. It was here, during this campaign which began with a disaster and ended with an unconditional victory, that the future Lord of the Admiralty, the future Minister of War, and the future Prime Minister, learned the value of time. In the course of the second World War, which the British call "Hitler's war" as they call the first World War "the Kaiser's war," Churchill illustrated the adage attributed to Napoleon: "I am prepared to give you everything you ask for, except more time." To believe that there will be time tomorrow to do what has not been done today is a fatal error and applies to the High Command as much as it does to the humblest private soldier. Time is a precious help only to the man who realizes how vital it is not to lose a second. Most men take *all* their time to do something which becomes impossible to carry out, for the simple reason that time was not on their side but on their adversary's side and the adversary acts as if time was escaping. Churchill learned this all-important lesson when he took part in the military operations in South Africa as a simple journalist.

He was now twenty-four years old and in the process of accumulating experience and that vast store of practical knowledge which would serve him in such good stead when the hour came for him to assume the supreme responsibility. His life was one long working day; he was working tirelessly to arm himself, equip himself in every way for that future which he carried inside himself, like the Spartan boy with his fox. It is only now that those who delve into his past can appreciate the importance of this period of his life. The marvel is that he himself should have known without a shadow of a doubt that it was essential for him to leave the beaten track, break all the rules, violate all the conventions in order to obey the not yet written law of his extraordinary genius. What did the South African War teach this unrecognized combatant, in spite of the orders and regulations of the War Office? It taught him to keep himself informed about everything, to take part in every action, to circumvent the regulations when he felt that he needed some new form of experience, to make an independent investigation of the consequences of issuing orders which could not be carried out because of lack of time. His account of his Boer War adventures in the *Morning Post* caused his name to become known all over the world. Further, he was paid a salary of £250 a month, plus expenses, and the paper also guaranteed him complete liberty of movement and opinion. He was now his own master, going where he liked, doing what he wanted, learning how to conduct himself when the hurricane of defeat seemed to be sweeping everything away. He learned where to plant his feet and brace himself when everything was going wrong, learned to appreciate the qualities of the rock on which the British Empire is built, particularly when he had nothing to cling to except his blind faith, which became greater day by day in his observation of the character of the British soldier at bay.

He landed at the Cape and leaped to the conclusion that the place to go to, because it was bound to be the main field of operations, was Natal, just invaded by the Boers. He took the train as far as Durban and then a little coastal steamer, intending to go to Ladysmith in spite of the fact that the Boers had surrounded it. There General Sir George White prepared his troops for a long siege. Churchill hastened to reach Eastcourt, seriously threatened by the enemy advance and the base for scouting patrols, which were being dispatched at frequent intervals to report on the movements of the Boers. These patrols were followed by mounted *estafettes* and it was, therefore, decided to use an armored train which would enable them to spot the advance enemy posts over a larger radius. The commander of the troops ordered to man the armored train happened to be a friend of Churchill's; he invited the *Morning Post* correspondent to join them as an observer. The offer was accepted enthusiastically. The train carried two infantry companies and a small cannon with its gun crew. The Boers ambushed the train and managed to run some of the trucks off the rails. The occupants of the train were surrounded and made an easy target for the Boer sharpshooters. In this emergency, although Churchill was considered technically a noncombatant, he abandoned his passive role without hesitation. He took over the command of the train. He set to work with the surviving troops, cleared the track, determined to save the engine, and loaded the wounded on to the tender. Then the locomotive returned, at full speed, to Eastcourt. Churchill was among those left behind on the track. As he was rallying the last of the men and making haste to find some sort of shelter, two

Boer horsemen appeared. A third galloped up almost immediately and forced the small group of unarmed men to surrender. The three horsemen, fingers on the triggers of their carbines, then marched War Correspondent Winston Churchill and his companions sixty miles, in the pouring rain, to Elandslaagte. From there they were sent by train, with other prisoners, to Pretoria.

On the way Churchill had time to reflect on his position and his probable fate. As a journalist, his papers were marked *Noncombatant*. Nevertheless, there was no gainsaying the fact that he had been caught in the act. At the first threat of danger, he had taken command and it was thanks to him, to his sense of timing and co-ordination, that while the Boers were trying to capture the train the British were able to save the wounded and recover the locomotive. He had tried to convince the Boer horseman who had taken him prisoner that there had been a misunderstanding as to his status; the man shook his head and answered, "We are not going to let you go, my fine fellow. You may only be a journalist, but it is not every day that we have the luck of putting our hands on the son of a lord!" At Pretoria, Winston Churchill found himself surrounded in the prison yard by sixty British officers who had been taken prisoner before him. For three weeks Churchill continued to protest against his imprisonment, calling heaven and the enemy authorities to witness that he was nothing but a journalist and should be set free at once. Unfortunately for him, those whose lives he had saved and who had returned to general headquarters sang his praises loudly for the heroic part he had played at the time of the armored train episode. The Natal newspapers wrote up his exploit in glowing terms. When the Boer general, Joubert, in command at Pretoria, read these articles he had young Churchill informed that, as he had taken command of the men who had succeeded in sending off the locomotive with its cargo of wounded, he had undoubtedly taken part in a military action and committed a breach of the recognized rules and should consider himself a prisoner of war.

COURAGE IN CAPTIVITY

LOOK for a way out; find it; use it. According to Churchill, courage in a prisoner consists in not staying in prison. Resignation is an attribute of sanctity, and the correspondent of the *Morning Post* was far from being a saint. Quite the contrary. At twenty-four, he had a devil in him. In his Pretoria prison, with his pencil as his sole weapon, Churchill would have been delighted to subscribe to the sentiments expressed by a witty Parisian, inadvertently locked up in Fresnes Prison as a political prisoner. Speaking to the warder, who, anxious to comply with the rules of the prison, wanted to take away the cane which he always carried, not because he was lame but because he was a dandy: "Oh no, if you take my cane away, I shall leave!"

Of all the thoughts which jostled each other in his head, which buzzed with history like an angry hive deprived of its queen, this was the thought that Churchill concentrated upon and became obsessed with: *Ask and it shall be given you; seek and ye shall find.* He had wasted three weeks demanding his immediate release by appealing to law and justice. More than enough. It was time to invoke the other, the divine justice. He would take his cause into his own hands; very completely, one can well believe. The prison in which Churchill was incarcerated with the other British officers was a model school which had been turned into a model prison. But it was not a suitable residence for a representative of the free press. He intended to prove this fact to his warders, his comrades, his colleagues in London, the censors at the War Office, his family, and to the world. If his jailers had had eyes to see they might well have suspected his intentions from his stance, his feet wide apart and squarely planted on the ground. The model prison of Pretoria was surrounded by barbed wire ten feet high and guarded, inside, by sentries armed to the teeth, posted fifty paces apart and patrolling their beats continuously.

Young Winston and two of his fellow prisoners had just made the discovery that they could watch the sentries from an opening in a latrine which the prisoners were allowed to use in the courtyard, and determine the exact moment at which a sentry had his back turned to a certain spot; this would solve their problem, the escape could start from that point. It should be possible for a man who was young and in training to jump over the fence, a difficult and dangerous undertaking, drop down on the other side and save himself from falling by a powerful twist of the wrist; then he would climb over the barbed wire and let himself drop into the garden on the other side, which was abandoned and overgrown with weeds. Churchill's first attempt failed, but fortunately the sentry did not see him fall back on the wrong side of the fence. He was determined to make another attempt, this time with his two friends. One after another, they were to jump over the formidable barrier which separated them from freedom. This time, Churchill took a long run and sailed over the fence. Crouching among the weeds, he waited for his two companions to follow his example. But his two friends wormed up to the other side of the fence as cautiously as Sioux Indians, to urge him to get away as quickly as possible, as the sentry was on the alert and had his carbine up to his shoulder. It is this incident which started the legend, so often exploited by Churchill's enemies when he returned to England, of his selfish escape, according to a plan agreed upon in common but carried out prematurely by him alone, thus making it impossible for the others to escape. Churchill's biographers have made short work of this calumny. They have all been at great pains to show the escape of the prisoner of Pretoria in its true light.

There can be no argument about it having been providential for England that Churchill was the one who escaped. But that he saved himself by a breach of trust, by deceit or malice, by depriving his comrades of their chances of freedom, is in flagrant contradiction of his generous character. Actually, he had cleared the ground for the other two, been the first to risk an untried method of escape for which each one of them had to rely on the rapidity of his reflexes and the degree of development of his instinct for self-preservation. Once on the other side, he waited for the two others and then followed their advice to be off as quickly as possible. He crawled from bush to bush across the garden which had reverted to a jungle. He then found a path; this led him to a lane, and he finally reached the main street of the town. Down this he strolled, like the born actor he is, and potential clown, his hands in his pockets, disheveled and poorly clad but nevertheless having a good look at the shop windows and the women. Without showing any signs of being in a hurry, he made for the railroad, which he knew would lead him in the direction of the frontier with neutral Portuguese territory.

He walked along the tracks and spied a supply train just shuddering into movement. He managed, not without difficulty, to jump on one of the open cars and lay down behind some sacks of coal. If a guard caught sight of him, he would be done for. Then he burst out laughing; he had thought of a story about a Jew, hidden during a pogrom in Russia behind some sacks filled with potatoes, who, when the soldiers came up to prod the sacks with their bayonets, could not help calling out: "Potatoes!"

He jumped off the train before dawn, afraid of being discovered in the daylight. When the train had lumbered off, he hid himself in a woods near the Portuguese frontier. It was here that the intervention of heaven became manifest. *Heaven helps those who help themselves*; young Churchill must be saved at all costs, after saving himself. He caught sight of a light in the distance; he approached the house, which proved to be the only one in the district still occupied by an Englishman, who had been left to look after a coal mine. His providential host took him down into the depths of a rat-infested cellar in which the fugitive remained hidden for several days. Thanks to providence he was thus able to stay in this unsalubrious retreat long enough to allow the sensation which his escape had caused to die down. The Boers had put a price on his head and advertised the fact by bill-posting the whole country; patrols were scouring the countryside; a reward was offered to anyone who would bring the fugitive back to Pretoria, dead or alive. The delightful sensation of being as notorious in absence as he usually was in person may, to some degree, have compensated him for the rats.

While he was crouching in his subterranean cave, living his recent adventures over again in his mind, his temporary protector was by no means idle; he was trying to find the safest way of passing his guest across the Portuguese frontier. On a day which should be marked by fortune, the war correspondent Winston Spencer Churchill reached the Portuguese port of Lourenço Marques at nightfall and hastened to make his presence known to the British Consul. As soon as they heard about his arrival, the whole British community rallied and offered its services. There was keen competition as to who should be the first to offer him a hot bath, present him with new clothes or a bottle of whisky, and the men organized a permanent bodyguard to prevent him from being kidnaped (they knew of the presence of enemy agents in the town and at the docks). A steamer was alongside the quay, bound for Durban, which was still in British hands. There was just time to board her, take leave of his savior and all those who had helped him and he was away. A few days later, he landed at Durban and reported at once to the military authorities. The commander-in-chief sent for him. At headquarters, he was asked to report on his observations while in the Transvaal. In the meantime he found that his escape, which had been due to his courage and his resourceful imagination, had aroused enormous interest and had been described in terms of the utmost enthusiasm in innumerable articles in the newspapers, not only in London but all over the British Empire; he was now the fashionable hero. His adventure served as an antidote to the depression which had overwhelmed the British nation during what was called the "Black Week" of the war in South Africa. There had been an unbroken succession of defeats during his detention: at Stormberg, at Magersfontein, and at Colenso, British troops had been defeated by the Boers. The general, after having interrogated the officer who preferred journalism to soldiering, ended the interview by expressing his admiration for the audacity and bravery which he had displayed in the course of the adventure.

"Is there anything we can do for you?" asked the general. Churchill, with the odor of powder and defeat in his nostrils, which, for obscure reasons, were not displeasing to him, as if they were his natural climate, replied without hesitation that he would like a temporary commission in the army, in the corps of volunteers which was being raised by the British in their South African territories. The general replied with equal promptness in the form of a question: "What about the *Morning Post*? What will you do about the *Morning Post*?" The answer was not long in coming: He was bound to his paper by a contract, which it would be dishonorable to break. The general sensed that the situation had changed and that it was no longer expedient to apply the rule which had been made for the precise purpose of taming young Churchill. Sir Redvers Buller decided to make an exception in favor of this same Churchill who had been responsible for all the trouble. He had to admit, however, that this professional rule-breaker deserved to be allowed to break yet another one. "Agreed," said the general, "you shall have your commission; and I am sure that you will do your best to carry out both your duties brilliantly." And then he added, as a Parthian shot: "But you will get no pay from us." Thus, once again Winston Churchill rejoined the forces in the field, serving gratuitously. He was appointed as lieutenant to a newly formed contingent of light cavalry, The South African Light Horse, and continued to send an avalanche of dispatches to the *Morning Post*. He continued in this dual capacity up to the relief of Ladysmith in the month of February 1900. He was invited to celebrate the event at headquarters. On this occasion, as he confessed later, some bottles of champagne, which had been jealously saved for him, were opened with great pomp and ceremony.

But the campaign dragged on inconclusively. A new commander-in-chief, Lord Roberts, had taken Buller's place. There was considerable difference of opinion among the senior officers about Churchill's articles in the *Morning Post,* owing to the vehement way in which he expressed his opinions and the postwar policy which he advocated. Lord Roberts was said to be particularly unappreciative of the young war correspondent's talents and independence. Moreover, Churchill happened to be his subordinate.

Thanks to the large number and influence of his friends, the commander-in-chief's objections had no disagreeable consequences for Churchill. So he left for the line of battle, equipped, thanks to the munificence of the *Morning Post*, with everything that a young officer could carry in the way of comforts and delicacies. He entered Pretoria as a conqueror.

The fall of Pretoria marked the end for Winston Churchill of this war, which he had begun as a civilian and finished once again in uniform. The prisoner had succeeded in escaping twice—once by jumping over barbed wire, the second time by jumping over the hurdle of a rule which forbade him from fighting on two fronts. And as everything in his life tends to be first-class material for some form of literary composition, it happened that the Boer horseman who captured him after his train exploit and made him walk sixty miles in the driving rain, turned out to be none other than General Botha. Three years after the war, when the Boer commanders were invited to London by their victorious adversaries, Churchill recognized the man who had made him prisoner.

This was the beginning of a prolonged and intimate friendship which developed with the years. Churchill and General Botha, both convinced that the danger of a war with Germany was increasing day by day, were converted from adversaries under the most dramatic circumstances to the best friends in the world. This is one of Churchill's forms of courage, as it is one of his most engaging qualities, to be able to put into practice, after the battle is over, the axiom so dear to Tolstoi: *To love one's enemies is a spiritual delight.* But the essential difference between the English genius and the Russian genius consists in this: To love one's enemy, but only on the condition of being the conqueror of the man who has once beaten you, and to know, afterwards, how to conquer oneself.

THE COURAGE TO BE A CONSERVATIVE

Ever since the Chaldean shepherds invented astronomy, the planets have been moving from left to right. The same applies to politicians. Let us return to the renegade who has just changed over from the professional army to journalism and who managed to combine the function of voluntary combatant with that of war correspondent. He returned to England with the intention of running for Parliament at the general election of 1900. For him the crucial question was what was his political attitude to be. He had been born on the right, so to speak, and yet was conscious of all the painful social and national problems which inevitably asserted themselves in an irresistible wave, moving from the multitude of the unfortunate toward the fortunate few.

Fresh from his experiences on the field of battle, young Churchill was spoiling for the electoral fray and impatient to mount the platform—it might almost be called the stage, as electioneering is essentially dramatic. His first stage appearance, face to face for the first time with the English electorate, was an important event in his life, for the great public were to be the judges, masters, adorers and even executioners upon whom he would depend for the rest of his life. The year is 1900. The century has changed its name. The overwhelming majority of the electors are still profoundly Conservative; the old Queen

97

is still on the throne. Nevertheless, things are not going as well as they were at the zenith of British prosperity when old Melbourne, that typical eighteenth-century man, said to his young sovereign in answer to her question: "My lord, what is going to happen?"—"Madame, nothing ever happens!"

But at the turn of the century a lot was happening— all the time. Young Churchill was introduced to the electors of the constituency of Oldham by Lord Dufferin in person, acting as sponsor.

At the general election of 1900, the voters of Oldham listened to Lord Randolph Churchill's son soliciting their votes, after hearing Lord Dufferin's introduction: "You see this young man! At his age, most of his contemporaries have not finished their studies, but he has been more often under fire and has already fought in more campaigns than a good half of the general officers commanding in Europe!" It was thus in the guise of a soldier, twenty-four years old but already wise in experience, like all those who have looked death in the face, that Winston Churchill was proclaimed the Conservative candidate and sent to Parliament by the electors of Oldham on Lord Dufferin's advice. The very term *conservative* might seem more appropriate to men whom the years have matured.

Young Lyautey, who resembled young Churchill in so many ways, once went to Rome as spokesman for the Conservative legitimists, to seek audience of the Pope. He went of his own accord to open his heart to the Universal Father, as the representative of Henri V. The Pope was then Leo XIII. Lyautey said: "Legitimism in France is not dead; and that is an opinion held not only by old gentlemen." The Holy Father gazed benignly at this young officer who had constituted himself the defender of fidelity to the Monarchy. Then the Holy Father, after reflecting for a moment, asked: "And how many are you, my son, who share this opinion in France?" Young Lyautey was perplexed; he searched his mind in vain for a figure and finished up by saying: "Very many . . . most Holy Father. Many more than one thinks . . ."— "My son! I know your country, better than you know it! Unfortunately, you are in a very small minority . . ." And the papal benediction had fallen, from the heights of eternal wisdom, on Lieutenant Lyautey's forehead.

Young Churchill's problem, as he took his seat on the Conservative benches, was quite the opposite. There were too many of them in England, both young and old— all Conservatives and legitimists to boot. There was nothing for a young Conservative who had just entered Parliament for the first time to do but share the opinions of the majority. The trumpet blasts of fame are still far distant and faint in the future. At that time that pale face, those pensive eyes, that mouth firmly closed on the secrets of the future, that condescending manner affected by Marlborough's descendant returned to live among his own people, inspired neither confidence nor liking in the leaders of the Conservative Party. The same applied to the majority of members on the benches around him. Churchill, for his part, felt very lukewarm toward these Tories on whose ship he had embarked, and in fact be-

lieved himself to be drowning. He had been entered for
the Conservative Party before he came into this world,
but now made up his mind that there were far too many
jostling each other on the benches, at the bar or in the cor-
ridors of Westminster. He had a sensation of being sub-
merged, first by the crowd of his electors and then by his
colleagues—perhaps also by their mediocrity.

He began meditating about what the Conservative
Party had done to his father; Lord Randolph died young
and in despair because he had not been able to fulfill his
self-appointed task of revitalizing the Conservative Party
from top to bottom. His son made no attempt to conceal the fact that he harbored the same ambition, if only
for the sake of vindicating his father, whom he admired
immensely—all the more since he had not succeeded in
doing what he set out to do because of his premature death. From the very beginning Churchill called
himself a Tory democrat, which might be said to mean
that he carried the twentieth century on his shoulders.
He had inherited from his father a taste, understanding,
and aptitude for public affairs, as if they were his own.
From his American mother he had inherited the instinct
for publicity, determination, and above all a sense of his
own personality. He was quite prepared to demonstrate
his abilities to the full without hesitating to draw attention to himself. In fact quite the contrary—he enjoyed
listening to speakers on his election platform extolling
his merits, and even added his own contribution to the
chorus of praise without worrying about the accusation
of blowing his own trumpet. His critics, of course,

claimed he blew it too loudly. In Parliament Churchill made his boredom with the proceedings only too obvious. He would sink down wearily on the benches of the House of Commons, a hunched-up figure, impatiently twiddling his watch chain. There was nothing to do, in the case of a young member of the party in power, except keep his mouth shut, and that for longer than this new recruit could tolerate. Life was much more enjoyable when he was risking death. One of his biographers has counted the number of times he was in danger of losing his life; the total figure is seven before he entered the political arena.

During Churchill's first four years in the Commons, when he did speak, his eloquence made little or no impression on the House; if he did succeed in attracting attention it was because of a slight fault in elocution which took him a long time to overcome, without ever succeeding—perhaps fortunately, because it enhances his originality—in doing away with it altogether. This fault consists in the imperfect pronunciation of the letter s.

Now that Churchill has become so eminent, the imitators of his style of delivery are innumerable; every student at Oxford or Cambridge has made the attempt. Everyone has repeated his epigrams, his sallies, his jokes, not to speak of the very individual manner in which he pronounced those grave words: "I have nothing to offer but blood, toil, tears and sweat." But in the early days with which we are still concerned, this young man became *persona non grata* to the Tories. When he rose to his feet to say a few words in debate, he could hear all around him the members of his own party imitating his faulty elocution, though it was impossible for the Speaker to detect the culprits responsible for this cruel and muffled form of baiting. More than once these tactics succeeded in forcing young Churchill to give up the struggle and sit down, livid with rage.

His attacks in the press on the Balfour Government caused a great stir and became increasingly popular with the public, though they were hardly calculated to consolidate his position in Parliament, or make it more agreeable. This strange label of "Tory democrat" which he had adopted revived in the minds of many the memory of Lord Randolph Churchill's struggles, which were still remembered vividly by the Conservative members. Some of the older members of the Party said of him in private, and sometimes in public, that he would become a second edition of his father—a brilliant but unstable man, a danger to those who had to work with him. Certain ill-disposed commentators in the press accused the son of an excess of filial devotion to the memory of the father. Lord Randolph Churchill had always been a rebel by temperament. In the earlier part of his career he was, like Disraeli before him, a Conservative in revolt, which, though it rendered a great service to the country, shook the confidence of the Conservatives in themselves. He was always appealing to them to bridge the abyss which separates the different classes, and insisting, with embarrassing pertinacity, in trying to transform a party which had always represented a single section of the community into a national party. Winston Churchill, when he adopted the same ideal and took up the battle against routine, egoism, and class prejudice which death forced his father to abandon, revived the fears, antipathies, and quarrels which had caused Lord Randolph to resign from the Conservative Party, only to disappear from the political stage, leaving behind him a brilliant track which the darkness of his premature death had not obliterated. Lord Randolph had risked his career for a great ideal; his son was determined to follow in his footsteps. If his father was a rebel he would be one too. Just as his father had never hesitated to fight the men of his own party, he would do so too.

In the case of some members, remorse was added to fear and dislike; it was not reassuring to have to face the son after betraying the father. The sincerity of his sentiments was questioned; was he really a Conservative? Or, by a duality which seemed the very essence of his nature, a democrat, or even a demagogue? All doubts were possible. He felt it beneath his dignity to attempt to dissipate any of them; he agreed with Stendhal (whom perhaps he had not read): *The more intelligent a man is, the less is he liable to be a good Party man.* In young Churchill, the courage to be a Conservative was soon going to be succeeded by that other form of courage which he would need to break with a long past and cease, for a time at least, to be a Conservative.

THE COURAGE TO DECLARE HIMSELF

ON MORE than one occasion, either in England, or in Italy or, more recently, in one of those charming resorts in the South of France, where people whose lives are finished or have not yet started congregate for the winter like birds seeking warmth, I have met an amiable old lady about whom a self-appointed commentator said to the other guests, "You know, Lady X, or Mrs. Y (who used to be a ravishing beauty) was once asked by Winston Churchill to marry him; she refused him several times . . ." and then added: "I believe that she has never forgiven herself!" I always refrained from asking for any further information. Something must be left for future authors who delve into the romantic life of the great Churchill.

Lord Winterton, who was re-elected to Parliament without a break from 1904 to 1951 when he retired of his own accord, represented his faithful electorate for forty-seven years as Conservative member, starting as the "Baby of the House" and finishing as the "Father of the House." During that time he had abundant opportunity for observing the phases and periods of popularity and unpopularity through which Winston Churchill passed in the course of his parliamentary career. At first, his career was neither easy nor agreeable, until the moment when that entity called the House surrendered to him, thankful to find, renewed in his person, its own highest traditions allied to every contradictory form of eloquence, to which neither his friends nor his enemies could remain insensible. Lord Winterton shows us a Churchill, at first irascible and vindictive, become suave, ironical or insulting, but never taking a mean advantage of an opponent, vehement and then profoundly humane; always able to hold the attention of the House, evoking in turn laughter, astonishment, disapproval and enthusiasm. And Winterton concludes, with perspicacity: "It will be difficult in the future for this man, very happily married to an exceptionally beautiful and charming woman and called upon, while still a young man, to fill one of the highest offices of the State (First Lord of the Admiralty), to go on believing that it is his mission in life to do battle with everybody, or in any case, with several thousand people guilty of having slighted his father and of having opposed his own ideas."

It was, therefore, a mollified Churchill, a happy Churchill that calamitous year 1914. He is a Minister; he is the fortunate husband of Clementine Hozier, a happy father, and an important member of Asquith's Liberal government, which had been elected with a substantial majority.

Forgotten are those other fair ones whose names were linked with his in country house drawing-room gossip in Yorkshire or Hertfordshire. How many hopeless love letters, signed by Winston, will our descendants inherit? There is no doubt that Churchill had been very susceptible to beauty in women. I shall give some examples which

I happen to have heard about. I can only guess at the others and I leave the subject to future historians. Let them describe Winston's heyday, his sentimental education, and the atmosphere of melancholy not unmixed with relief caused by his early rebuffs. There will be no lack of chroniclers to write the book of beautiful listeners who dismissed him.

On one occasion only did Churchill succumb to the temptation of pouring out his heart on paper by writing a novel called *Savrola*. In this book he writes about an imaginary country, in which he describes the course of an adventure which is partly romantic and partly political. He wrote it at the age of twenty-three and it suggests that he was dominated by these two governing passions. He dedicated this novel, a premature flowering of his powerful imagination, to the officers of the 4th Hussars "in whose company the author lived for four happy years." It was first published as a serial in *Macmillan's Magazine*; when it appeared in book form, the author wrote a Preface: *And now I submit it to the judgement or clemency of the public.*

The hero, Savrola in person, bears a striking likeness to the author. He is described as a representative of the party of the people and of liberty against tyranny, at dagger point with a dictator. The scene is laid in Laurania, a Mediterranean republic, five years after a civil war. The president, Antonio Molara, after establishing a dictatorship with the help of the armed forces, holds the country in his iron grip, in a manner which has become only too familiar to us. Here we have Savrola in his armchair, meditating; the revolution has just broken out and the first victory has been won, leaving on the square in front of the president's palace "forty bodies and some expended cartridges lying on the ground." And here is the description of Savrola's state of mind:

His nervous temperament could not fail to be excited by the vivid scenes through which he had lately passed, and the repression of his emotion only heated the inward fire. Was it worth it? The struggle, the labour, the constant rush of affairs, the sacrifice of so many things that make life easy, or pleasant—for what? A people's good! That, he could not disguise from himself, was rather the direction than the cause of his efforts. Ambition was the motive force and he was powerless to resist it. He could appreciate the delights of an artist's life devoted to the search for beauty, or of sport, the keenest pleasure that leaves no sting behind. To live in a dreamy quiet and philosophic calm in some beautiful garden, far from the noise of men and with every diversion that art and intellect could suggest, was, he felt, a more agreeable picture. And yet he knew that he could not endure it. Vehement, high and daring was his cast of mind. The life he lived was the only one he could ever live, he must go on to the end.

The critics pointed out that the novel, which contained no fewer than 70,000 words, was written while the author was on active service in India. In view of the manner in which the story develops in the ensuing chapters we are justified in indulging in the gentle sport of *cherchez la femme*: the heroine is called Lucile: naturally, she is young and beautiful; we meet her the day after the outbreak of the rebellion, the first open manifestation of the people's discontent with their dictator. She is the dictator's wife. We see her, sitting down at the breakfast table, not saying a word, facing her husband. The author writes, "She tactfully refrained from irritating him by the laboured commonplaces of matutinal conversation."

The president's habit was to start work at nine o'clock in the morning. Lucile decided to go for a ride in her carriage because she considered it her duty, after what had happened the day before, to show her courage by facing the public. "It might help her husband, for her beauty was such that an artistic people showed her respect."

The end of the story shows us the dictator, unscrupulously exploiting his wife's beauty to deter Savrola from his determination to overthrow the dictatorship; the final scenes are concerned with the partial success of the insurgents, followed by the violent though natural death of the dictator, the exile of the beautiful Lucile, the counterrevolution and the triumph of democracy—all this rushed through in record time. The final climax shows the people's ingratitude toward Savrola, their savior. Thoroughly disgusted, he joins his beloved Lucile in exile. There is an epilogue which throws a curious light on the young novelist, who is soon to give up novel writing in favor of history:

Those who care to further follow the annals of the

Republic of Laurania may read how, after the tumult had subsided, the hearts of the people turned again to the illustrious exile who had won them freedom and whom they had deserted in the hour of victory. Those who may scoff at the fickleness of men, may read of the return of Savrola and his beautiful consort to the ancient city he had loved so well.

This figment of his imagination which appears under the name of Lucile may well bear some relationship to one of those charming old ladies who were said to have been "sought in marriage" by Churchill. What I find significant, for my part, and which I consider worthy of being added to the Churchillian folklore, is the clear exposition of his cult for feminine beauty, which still constitutes for him the supreme quality in women.

Sir Edward Marsh was one of Churchill's early friends, and he knew and served him better than any of his other contemporaries. He described young Churchill and young Edward Marsh, ensconced behind a gold-encrusted door to the ballroom; through this, the famous beauties of the waning Victorian era and the dawning Edwardian era passed under the crossfire of their admiring looks, as they shook hands with their hostess before advancing into the ballroom. The two young men, both of them soaked in classical literature, invented a game inspired by Marlowe's lines describing the beauty of Helen of Troy:

Was this the face that launch'd a thousand ships
And burnt the topless towers of Ilium!

As each celebrated beauty entered the room, they called out a number to each other—the number of ships they would be prepared to launch to make a conquest of the lady in question. The first fair lady passed:

"Five hundred," murmured Churchill generously.

"No, only four hundred and fifty," corrected Marsh, who was more difficult to please. But when it came to Lady Helen Vincent, the future First Lord of the Admiralty assessed her at a thousand ships, without a shadow of a doubt. Eight to nine hundred was the figure for the Duchess of Rutland, and a thousand, unhesitatingly so, for that marvel of marvels: the legendary Duchess of Sutherland—Lady Millicent—whose beauty attracted regiments of admirers without her meaning to. It was from her own lips that I learned something about Churchill as he was during the years of his sentimental apprenticeship.

The Duchess of Sutherland was in the habit of giving a weekly ball at Stafford House, her London residence, throughout the season which, at that time, lasted three months. Her husband the duke, much older than she was, carefully scrutinized the invitations sent out by his wife, whom he knew to be of an adventurous and Liberal turn of mind. He himself was a Tory of the old school, a real die-hard and enemy of all innovations, who already had good reason to believe that things would not always continue as they were. Though he sat in the Upper House, he condescended to take an interest in the Commons, in which the pursestrings are manipulated, sometimes in a dangerously incompetent manner! When some young Conservative members, most of them either his relatives or sons of his friends, voted "wrong" in the Commons, that is to say contrary to his wishes, the old duke had a very simple way of punishing them: he made sure that they did not receive an invitation to the balls given by his wife. The duchess sometimes proved refractory, if the voting had taken place a short time before the given ball. But a husband of his sort knows how to enforce his decisions, however absurd they might be to a person of Liberal leanings. Further, Lady Sutherland was much averse to offending her friends.

In the duchess's own words: "One day, two of my dancers had voted on the wrong side. My husband insisted upon my writing to each of them, requesting them not to use the invitations I had sent them to my ball, for reasons which, in my opinion, were extremely embarrassing and which I intended to explain later. I was exasperated at having to write these letters, but my husband was adamant and I could not refuse. One of the members, whose invitation I canceled reluctantly, was Lord Hugh Cecil, son of Lord Salisbury, the Prime Minister, and the other was Winston Churchill. I still have in my possession the letters they wrote to me in reply. I kept them because they were so characteristic of these two contrasting temperaments. Hugh Cecil wrote: 'My dear Millie, I understand and I am sorry. Will you do me a great favour and tell me what day next week you will be free to have lunch with me . . . ?' As to Winston, who was entirely lacking in the proverbial urbanity of the Cecils, he wrote such an angry letter that it made me laugh, declaring roundly that he would not set foot in my house as long as the duke lived."

THE COURAGE TO BE A LIBERAL

THE service for the first Sunday in Advent contains these words: *The virtues of heaven shall be shaken.* I think of them when I look at old photographs which show across the years, the face of the young Churchill, Member of Parliament. I did not know him at the time, but many friends and members of my family have pictured him to me as he was at the time of the election at Dundee, on May 14, 1908. Then, not yet thirty, he had ceased to gravitate inside the orbit of the Conservatives and had three years before decided to change parties.

Asquith, leader of the Liberals after an overwhelming victory at the elections, had just appointed Winston Churchill President of the Board of Trade. A short time previously, instead of remaining a Tory democrat, he had declared himself a Liberal. His father had attempted to combine the two, he had been an advanced Conservative, commonly called a progressive. But he had been unsuccessful. To go from right to left seems contrary to the nature of things, whereas to go from left to right seems to succeed almost always.

Young Churchill, for his part, considered himself more advanced than was healthy for someone to remain associated with the Right-wing Conservatives. Churchill decided to risk his whole career, just to take those few steps which separate the Conservative from the Liberal benches. Accompanied as he was by the shadow of his father, changing sides was a truly dangerous procedure. Not only was his reputation at stake; the very foundations of his character, his good faith, would be doubted. For a long time, he would be suspect in both camps, perhaps always. All Asquith's authority would be required to make him acceptable to his Cabinet, and even more so to the rank and file of the Party at the next elections. In the ranks of the Conservatives, whom he left some time before their resounding defeat, he was being accused publicly of having abandoned the Conservative Party because Balfour had waited too long before appointing him to a Cabinet post. Why was he so impatient for power? Soon the real reason would become known, but no one had any inkling as yet. The widely held opinion, unfortunately, among members of both parties was that Churchill would do anything to get into the Government. The ambitious young man was denounced for being tired of champing at the bit and, because he had found the path to power too obstructed on the right, had therefore decided on a short cut, even to the extent of walking across that intangible boundary which separates the two sides of the House, sacrosanct to any honest Englishman.

The two sides of the House are separated physically by nothing but a few square feet of green baize carpet, the real purpose of which is to deaden the sound of the footsteps of the honorable Members as they come forward in turn to bow before the no-longer-existent altar of the Chapel of St. Stephen. Here you have the mystical element, the real presence. This salute is addressed, not to the arbiter in a wig, the Speaker who sits under the canopy and moderates parliamentary debates, but to an invisible divinity. The unforgettable words of an old French priest, the Abbé Mugnier, on the occasion of his visit to Parliament, throw a vivid light on that scene of young Churchill's crossing the House: "It is not surprising that politics are a religion in England, seeing that you practice them in a church!" In crossing the green carpet, Lord Randolph's son not only changed his party, at his risk and peril, but also transgressed a moral law; he was conscious that he had become a sign of the times; like the storm-bird, he was an indication of where the deluge would come from. The ancient Greeks claimed that future events overtake us before we overtake them; the dates which mark the different stages of Winston Churchill's destiny are already preordained. His decision conferred a spurious plausibility upon the allegations of those who attribute the basest motives to his action; all is fair in love and war. He is vituperated, vilified, scoffed at, and pilloried as a traitor, a term for which the political press had a singular predilection; the general disapproval of his own social stratum reflected, perhaps, among the Conservatives their regret at having lost him. His defection was conspicuous; he himself is always conspicuous. Ever since he walked his dogs in the streets of Harrow, contrary to the established rule of the school, he had been a kind of new Alcibiades to the Athenians.

In family albums and old illustrated magazines we

see him as he was at that time: the effects of exposure to the sun in India and the Sudan have worn off and his face has resumed its habitual pallor; his forehead, from which the hair has receded prematurely, shines like an alabaster lamp lit from within; even his figure has changed—this Queen's hussar, this victor of the polo tournament, is heavier and thicker-set. Ever since he began sitting in the House, his caricaturists have emphasized his singular posture; at rest, he suggests the profound gestation of some fabulous bird in the process of hatching something, the beak closed and the eyes half-shut; we find a simile in Shakespeare: *the phoenix fashioning his nest from the burning ashes of his sire.*

In the process of writing Lord Randolph Churchill's biography, that admirable book now considered a classic, Winston Churchill could meditate at his leisure on the tragedy of being born on the right with an urge to go toward the left in order to save what one loves. When one plunges into a flooded river, it is no longer a question of swimming against the current, but simply of avoiding being drowned. He knew by heart the words of his father's political testament. When he resigned, at the end of his tether, with death approaching, Lord Randolph wrote his despairing confession: "In dealing the Old Guard this fatal and final blow, I know that I am inflicting a mortal wound upon myself, but the deed is done." The Conservative Party will be liberalized and in consequence the Tories will once more become a powerful governing force. The son, his father's intellectual and spiritual heir, did not hesitate to make sure that the Party kept moving in the right direction by even more explicit methods. He understood that the danger no longer lay in the now obsolete division between Whigs and Tories, between Liberals and Conservatives. As Sir John Simon pointed out in his penetrating study "Churchill's Liberalism":

> Young Churchill had grasped this fact of incalculable importance: that we are now faced with two rival political credos; on the one side, the Liberals who believe in individual liberty, on the other side, a new Party who believe in the principle of a monstrous State to take the place of human beings in everything, quite indifferent to human dignity and which declares itself the sole master of all property in the hands of the State, controlled by the State, which arrogates to itself the absolute right of life or death over every individual in the nation, thus over the whole nation.

Young Churchill expressed his conception of this antithesis in a public speech which marked a date in the history of political parties in England. On the 14th of May 1908, in the course of the election at Dundee, he defined it in a manner which leaves behind him all the old arguments which Liberals and Conservatives hurled at each other throughout the nineteenth century. All that is finished, old-fashioned, obsolete, deserving neither tears nor regrets: "Liberalism," cried the new Liberal member, "has its own history and its own tradition. Socialism has its own formulas and aims. Socialism seeks to pull down wealth; Liberalism seeks to raise up poverty. Socialism

117

would destroy private interests. Liberalism would preserve private interests in the only way in which they
can be safely and justly preserved, namely, by reconciling
them with public right. Socialism would kill enterprise.
Liberalism would rescue enterprise from the trammels
of privilege and preference. Socialism assails the pre-
eminence of the individual. Liberalism seeks and shall
seek more in the future, to build up a minimum standard
for the mass. Socialism exalts the rule; Liberalism exalts
the man. Socialism attacks capital. Liberalism attacks
monopoly."

Forty years later, the Liberal Sir John Simon declares
that the Liberal policy, as it was formulated by young
Churchill, still stands as the only adequate definition of
his program and that of his Party.

But the young prodigy in the field of prophecy who
has foreseen everything, had already provided clear
evidence of his genius for politics in general when, as far
back as 1906, he put before the House of Commons a plan
to guarantee the autonomy of the Transvaal and the Or-
ange Free State. In an inspired and bold speech, forestall-
ing the most advanced ideas which were to be accepted
only after another half-century, the young Under-
Secretary explained and justified the Liberal government's policy. In a pathetic appeal to the Conservative
opposition he pleads with his old leaders and all the members of the Conservative Party to support the treaty, because it depends upon them whether it remain a sterile

Party victory or a spontaneous gift from the united nation. This was how he expressed himself:

"I address myself particularly to the right honorable gentlemen who sit opposite, who are long versed in public affairs and who will not be able all their lives to escape from a heavy South African responsibility. They are the accepted guides of a Party which, though in a minority in this House, nevertheless embodies nearly half the nation. I will ask them seriously whether they will not pause before they commit themselves to violent or rash denunciations of this great arrangement. I will ask them, further, whether they cannot join with us to invest the grant of a free constitution to the Transvaal with something of a national sanction. With all our majority we can only make it the gift of a Party; they can make it the gift of England!"

The survivors of the old Liberal Party and of that past, which is now dead and gone, will not fail to bear witness to those heroic times, when the passionate voice of young Churchill was the first to be raised in defense of the right of governments to self-determination, always within the limits of their wisdom on the one hand and their own instincts for self-preservation on the other hand.

"At the present time," writes Lord Simon, already quoted, "we see in Sir Winston Churchill, leader of the Conservative Party, the man who was able to fulfil his father's dearest wish, by insufflating the spirit of English

119

Liberalism into that Party which he was to lead through storm and stress along the road to democracy." And he adds philosophically: "The content of political doctrines changes with time."

But in a deeper sense, Lord Simon was right in saying that in the person of Sir Winston Churchill, Prime Minister of a Conservative government, we still find the same young Liberal as before, the man chosen by Asquith.

Part Three

THE COURAGE TO FACE THE
GENERAL STRIKE

IN THE early morning of Tuesday, May 4, 1926, a small group of men could be seen going into the back door of the *Morning Post* building in London, not far from the Strand. They disappeared up a narrow staircase. A general strike had been declared. The men were Winston Churchill, Chancellor of the Exchequer, followed by some of his Cabinet colleagues and the heads of their respective departments. Ten minutes later, Churchill had become editor-in-chief of a new newspaper called the *British Gazette*. The editor-in-chief himself signed the government permit authorizing the publication of the paper. It was universally agreed that England was threatened in its essential activities by a domestic crisis more serious than any it had been called upon to face since the civil war, that is to say the struggle between the Stuarts and Parliament. The leaders of the strike thought that their cause was already victorious because they had succeeded in causing a total stoppage in the printing of newspapers. Not a single paper was to appear; strangely, the majority of the compositors were against striking, but they were afraid of disobeying trade union orders. In fact, small groups of compositors had continued printing till the very last moment, hoping to persuade their union leaders to allow them to go on working peacefully at their machines. Not only the proprietors of the great national newspapers but also the Government were well aware of the danger of allowing the suppression of all news. Radio was not yet widespread. Such circumstances gave the lie to the proverb: No news is good news! Rumors and distorted news were circulating. The public was ignorant of what was really happening and frightened by its own ignorance. There was near-panic and doubt was spreading through the whole country. The leaders of the strike were counting on this sequence of events and hoping that the public would soon show signs of being ripe for revolution—fear and blind submission to events which individuals believe that they can no longer control. The masses were already agitated by uncertainty and fear for the morrow.

It was then that England found the man capable of taking public opinion in hand and raising national morale: Churchill. Throughout the afternoon and the evening of the day before, the managing directors of the principal newspapers had been holding a meeting, but with no result, to try to come to an arrangement which would permit the pooling of their resources and the issuing of a single paper, for the purpose of preventing a panic and dissipating anxiety.

They were in fact paralyzed by the incompatibility of viewpoint between the parties which their papers represented. They separated without having succeeded in coming to any sort of agreement. One of them, H. A.

Gwynne, the editor-in-chief of the *Morning Post*, dissatisfied with this negative result, did not hesitate to find a solution and was prepared to take the entire responsibility on his own shoulders. He wrote a letter to the Government, offering his offices, the services of his employees and editorial staff and all the facilities at his disposal. At once the Prime Minister, Stanley Baldwin, so often in later years accused of negligence and inertia, called on the man capable of dominating the situation. Baldwin sent for Churchill. Later, his biographers did not fail to emphasize the significance of this fact, of which the whole of England was aware: In case of trouble and danger to the nation, the one and only remedy was Churchill! I need hardly say that the Chancellor of the Exchequer had never before set foot in a machine room where his articles were being printed. But what has always distinguished him from the more or less eminent men who gravitated around his orbit, was precisely this singular aptitude for applying himself to any task however extraordinary, provided that everybody else had given it up as a bad job; he was only interested in taking a situation in hand if it seemed desperate.

The amazed editors of the *Morning Post* saw Churchill, in spite of his ministerial responsibilities, appear that same night in the editorial sanctum. Never before had an editor-in-chief spent so many hours over the composing table. The editor of the newborn *British Gazette* divided his time largely between the machine room and the composing room, leaning over the shoulders of the small staff.

The first obstacle, insurmountable in the opinion of the

timid members of the Cabinet, was not long in showing itself. The Trade Unions forbade the few printing workers who had remained at their posts to go on working in the *Morning Post* building for a paper edited by the Government. Beric Holt, at that time one of the sub-editors of the *Morning Post*, was present and has described the atmosphere of impenetrable gloom. Churchill, with Gwynne, the old editor-in-chief, at his side, stood near the door watching the workmen disappearing one by one into the fog just before dawn. Some of these men had tears in their eyes as they filed past. Churchill lost no time in shaking off his depression. He put through a telephone call to his friend Max Beaverbrook; half an hour later, the head compositor of the *Daily Express* arrived. He sat down in front of the linotype and set the machine in motion. Churchill supervised and dictated the contents. The first edition of the *British Gazette* consisted of two printed pages, front and back; the two inside pages were left blank. Churchill watched every detail of the process. The question of distributing the paper was the next problem. Churchill did not hesitate, once more he had a stroke of genius. He appealed to the Automobile Club for volunteers. A mad rush, all over London, ensued. The sheets distributed that first morning were snatched from the volunteers' hands before they could reach the newsstands. The new editor-in-chief spent the whole afternoon converting this chaos into order. Nothing was forgotten: the crew of a submarine was brought up from Devonport to man the machines; students from London University volunteered to work the linotypes; Churchill appointed Admiral Hall as chief of the staff, as well as officer in charge of general security. Day and night an enormous crowd assembled in front of the building in which the *British Gazette* was being printed under these strange conditions.

Some of the crowd hooted and groaned. The same element tried to organize a storming of the premises, in order to stop the volunteers from working and to wreck the machines. Churchill sent for the police. There were a few isolated incidents of an unpleasant nature such as attacks on the volunteers as they left the building. To protect them, he called on the Irish Guards to reinforce the police.

The second night, when he went down to the machine room, he had the satisfaction of seeing that all the linotypes were working at full speed. He noticed some enamel jugs on the ground.

"What is in those jugs?" asked Churchill, whose curiosity had been aroused.

"Beer, sir," was the answer.

"Is there enough of it?" asked Churchill.

"Oh yes, sir, plenty!"

"Enough? You mean not enough," answered the editor-in-chief, "send for another lot, and then another one!"

That night 507,000 copies were pulled off the machines, as opposed to 232,000 on the previous night. For fear of sabotage, a purple card was distributed, without which no one was allowed into the building where the *British*

Gazette was being printed. Even Churchill was careful to carry it with him when he left the House of Commons or his office, and submitted it to the scrutiny of the guards on duty where this paper, unique not only in England but in the whole Empire, was being printed.

In the House of Commons, there were loud and vehemently expressed protests on the part of the members of the opposition that Churchill should be allowed to combine the contradictory functions of M.P., member of the Government, and editor-in-chief. In his defense, it was claimed that he managed, in some miraculous manner, to avoid neglecting any of his parliamentary or ministerial duties and, nevertheless, spent hours attending to editorial details. The Socialists naturally complained bitterly at the flagrant partiality of the articles published by the *British Gazette.* "The State cannot remain impartial when it is contending with a minority of its citizens," retorted Churchill. The opposition reply was to renew its attacks. The Labour members scoffed at the idea of confusing the Baldwin Government with the State and claimed that the strikers represented the State, as they constituted a majority in the population. This statement drew one of those crushing retorts from Churchill, for which he is never at a loss. He returned the compliment with a single sentence, which has become a classic:

"I refuse to be impartial when the fire brigade is fighting the fire!"

Soon, his adversaries ceased their diatribes. This fact, combined with the hourly reports he received from all parts of the country, convinced him that the general strike was fizzling out. He returned to his editorial office at the *British Gazette* and penned the following lines:

> Every man who does his duty by the country and returns to work will be protected by the State from the loss of Trade Union benefits or pension. His Majesty's Government will take whatever steps are necessary in Parliament or otherwise for this purpose.

This declaration was signed by the Prime Minister. It appeared in heavy print, at the top of the first page of the *British Gazette*; that edition sold the record number of 2,209,000 copies. The order to strike was rescinded. It had lasted seven days and nights. That night, Churchill sat in the editorial chair for the last time. The desk in front of him was covered with messages from all over the country and appeals for moderation sent by prominent politicians, even those who had been bitterly opposed to his policy during the crucial period of his brief career as editor-in-chief. He left the building, which now reverted to the *Morning Post*, as he came, without drums or trumpets. As an enthusiastic theatregoer and feeling the need of an hour or two of relaxation, he proceeded to the Empire Theatre in Leicester Square, where the musical comedy *Lady Be Good* was running.

He had taken his seat in the stalls after the play had started. Nobody had seen him come into the auditorium. Suddenly, someone recognized him and the whole audience started shouting: "We want Winston!" and rose to its feet. The singer on the stage stopped short and took a few steps toward the footlights; the lights came up in the auditorium. "There he is!" cried the actress, pointing at Churchill. "Three cheers for Winston Churchill!" roared the audience. Then the singer signaled to the conductor and cried: "God save the King!" The audience calmed down as if by enchantment, listened to the National Anthem in silence, and then joined in singing the last few lines.

No one had been more profoundly conscious of the danger than Churchill. He had grasped, as no one else had, the fact that the publication of reassuring news would have an eminently stabilizing effect; even on two pages out of four, leaving the other two blank. Almost immediately afterwards, soccer matches were organized all over the country between the erstwhile strikers and the police. The public followed them with enormous interest. These games were the British people's answer to those who had tried to divide them against each other.

A short time after the general strike, Churchill, on the ministerial bench, was again attacked by his Socialist adversaries. They harassed him and interrupted his speech. He stopped short, turned toward the Socialists, his eyes flashing fire, and said to them: "I warn you . . ." There was a deathly silence in the House. "I warn you," he continued slowly, "that if you ever attempt to start another general strike . . ." He took his time, seemed to be collecting his thoughts. Everyone, adversary and friend alike, was anxiously waiting for the final blow, wondering what thunderbolt he would launch to annihilate his opponents. But the whole House burst into laughter when Churchill concluded with a smile: "I shall set my dogs on you and publish a second *British Gazette!*"

THE COURAGE TO BE A PROPHET

EVEN as a young man Churchill had the gift of vision and prophecy, and it has kept him young. To be able to see into the future is an aptitude which comes from heaven. Let us listen to what G. W. Stevens says of young Churchill visited by the spirit of prophecy. Stevens was the *Daily Mail* war correspondent, a man of understanding, and Churchill's shipmate when he was returning to England after the Battle of Omdurman. He had been astonished to find that Churchill knew so much at the age of twenty-four, but only about things that would be useful to him, and have, in fact, been used by him when the right moment came. It is equally astonishing today to read what this journalist wrote, more than fifty years ago, about his young fellow traveler. The article appeared in the *Daily Mail*, under a title which was in itself prophetic, "The Youngest Man in Europe."

Stevens' analysis of young Churchill's character starts with his pedigree, which can be considered a code for deciphering the characters of illustrious men. We must go back to Marcus Aurelius, the most Athenian of Roman emperors, for a precedent. He used his heredity to explain his actions: "From my father, I inherit . . . from my mother . . . from my grandfather . . . from my ancestor . . ." followed by a list of the good and bad qualities of his maternal and paternal stock. In the same way, Stevens explains Churchill. He starts by saying: "Churchill is what he is by breeding." That is the key word.

In years he is a boy; in temperament he is also a boy; but in intention, in deliberate plan, purposive adaptation of means to ends he is already a man. But Churchill is a man, with ambitions fixed, with the steps towards their attainment clearly defined, with a precocious, almost uncanny judgement as to the efficacy of the means to the end. From his father he derives the hereditary aptitude for affairs, the grand style of entering upon them, which are not the less hereditary in British noble families because they skip nine generations out of ten. W. S. Churchill can hardly have seen much of Government and Parliament and foreign politics at twenty-four, but he moves in and out among their deviations with the ease, if not with the knowledge, of a veteran statesman. But that inheritance alone would not give him his facility. From his American strain he adds to this a keenness, a shrewdness, a half-cynical, personal ambition, a natural aptitude for advertisement, and, happily, a sense of humour.

That is what might be called a sixth sense: a sense of humor, which cannot be kept out of any conversation in England. It saves the English from being suffocated by tradition, and renders public life endurable with all its tragedy, because there is a parallel between grandeur and tragedy in the history of nations. Churchill is also a sybarite. When circumstances permit, he will give us ample proof of it, without any hypocritical attempts to conceal it.

I once dined with Sir Stafford Cripps at the British Ambassador's house in Romania, when he was on his way from Greece to Moscow in 1940. I could see that he was a rigid vegetarian. For this reason, I was particularly amused by Churchill's quip, as it was told to me several years later by Mrs. Leo Amery, wife of the ex-Secretary of State for India. The scene was the Turkish Embassy, toward the end of the second World War. The representative of Ankara, the capital of a neutral country, was not subject to rationing or other restrictions. He gave a dinner in honor of the Prime Minister, which included Bosporus lobsters, turkey, asparagus with hot butter sauce, and Floating Island for dessert, all dishes which had long since disappeared from London dinner tables, even official ones. The Prime Minister did not miss a mouthful. Stafford Cripps, his colleague, was seated opposite him— a vegetarian, a sort of ascetic Socialist monk. Churchill was rolling the mouthfuls of turkey and asparagus around his tongue; between two of the courses, he leaned over toward the lady on his right, glanced mischievously at his colleague who had refused every savory dish, one after the other, and said, "I am glad I am not a herbivore," and added, "I eat what I like, I drink what I like, I do what I like. . . ." Then, after a short silence, the will-o'-the-wisp glinting in his eyes, he concluded: "And he's the one to have a red nose!"

He may be a prophet, but no one can say that he has been the kind of prophet who retires into the desert and feeds on locusts and wild honey. He likes luxury, comfort, good food, and openly boasts of the fact. It is equally true that he has sometimes profoundly shocked Englishmen of his own class by his "stunts" and sartorial eccentricities, such as his passion for exotic hats. His singular taste for foreign decorations was mentioned by Stevens in his article and quoted by Churchill's biographers fifty years after it was written. Stevens related how Marshal Martinez Campos had bestowed on young Churchill the Order of Military Merit for his participation in the fight on Spain's side in Cuba. Churchill had not only accepted the order with enthusiasm, but was proud of it. It should be remembered that the first Elizabeth had promulgated the law (which is still in force) forbidding her subjects to wear foreign orders. She explained her reasons pithily: "I mark my pigs myself!" According to this law, the said pigs, whoever they are and right up to the present time, have to ask their sovereign's permission before allowing a foreign order to be pinned on their breasts. How many times since the Cuban war, one wonders, has young Churchill had to ask his sovereign's permission? And what would the angry Queen Bess, who destroyed the Armada, have thought of this Spanish Order, which he proudly bears—the first of many? And what, one also wonders, did Lady Randolph Churchill think when she saw her beloved son wearing the decoration, won fighting the troops of her motherland, America? "He who loves dearly, chastises pitilessly!" Jenny Churchill's son would become half-American once more when he signed the Atlantic Charter; and he would be present, his eyes glistening with tears, at the inauguration of a plate put up in America on the house where his mother was born.

"He is ambitious and calculating, but never in cold blood, and that is his saving grace," wrote Stevens as the result of his observations on the boat which brought this twenty-four-year-old Caesar and his fortunes back to England. According to this same writer, merit, energy and luck are the principal factors which allowed him to make his dreams come true so often and soar on the wings of his fancy, more often, perhaps, than any other man in this world. Stevens recapitulates this brief career already so singularly blessed by success: he was under fire on the frontier of India; he fought in Cuba; he entered Pretoria twice, first on a bicycle as a civilian, more precisely as a spy, the second time as a military conqueror; he won the polo cup in India; he charged at the head of his squadron, in order to be able to enter Khartoum as a conqueror. Now, on the way back, he was writing a book, as one would expect him to do; he finished it before the boat docked, which did not prevent him from preparing three political speeches at the same time, which he intended to deliver shortly after his arrival. He fascinated, dazzled and made a lifelong friend of his traveling companion, who noted the variability of his moods, which change with extraordinary frequency and suddenness, his lightning repartee, his long tirades and his love of quoting almost anything which his infallible memory dictated. Thank God, he was usually good-tempered. Twitted by his companion on his invariable and obvious self-satisfaction, Churchill laughed and gave a simple explanation: "I am young." He could be irritating and even maddening; usually because of his violent diatribes and his unbounded self-confidence, which verged on arrogance, but then he disarmed his audience by some humorous remark. Stevens, who was the first of his biographers, only noted essentials in this brief study, but still managed to throw much light on the fundamental qualities of this man of destiny. He goes so far as to say: "He has not studied to make himself a demagogue. He was born a demagogue and he happens to know it. At present he calls himself a Tory democrat. Tory, the opinions— might change; democrat, the methods—never. For he has the twentieth century in his marrow." Finally, Stevens asks himself:

> What will he become, who shall say? At the rate he goes there will hardly be room for him in Parliament at thirty or in England at forty. It is a pace that cannot last, yet already he holds a vast lead over his contemporaries. In the meanwhile he is a wonder—a boy with a man's ambitions and—more wonderful yet —a very mature man's self-appreciation—knowledge of his own powers and the extent to which each may be applied to set him forward on his road.

What road? The road to great destinies, which Marcus Aurelius called "the obstacle," until the moment of the miracle when the ambitious man finds that "the obstacle has become the road." Here we have the prophecies made about him at the age of twenty-four, about Churchill who will become a prophet in his turn and a prophet of gloom at that, as I shall bear witness when the time comes. It is a good thing that he was born a sybarite, that he has loved life; otherwise, since he has the terrible gift of seeing into the future, he could not have survived. The ancient Greeks considered this gift to be closely allied to madness, doubtless to restrain those who possessed it from committing suicide.

Sir Winston Churchill understands his own epoch, but he has an equally good understanding of the epochs which have preceded him. It is this which so profoundly differentiates him from the other politicians of his time, who have strutted across the stage of this world. He is neither superficial nor elementary, in contrast with all the others who have prided themselves on being able to rule and foresee and to have always been right (even when the gods themselves have been mistaken). When he began to divine the future—and it was very early in his career—he was so young that no one would believe him. On two separate occasions the forces of stupidity leagued against him.

Alone or almost alone, Churchill made predictions from the very beginning of the 1914 war. He had in his pocket at the time the secret report of a young staff officer, Colonel C. B. Thomson, who had been sent by the War Office to the Balkans, first as an observer in the first and second Balkan wars, and then for the purpose of rallying around the Christian standard all those scattered and divided countries of ancient Romania. He was the sort of man who was peculiarly fitted by nature to understand Churchill and be understood by him. These two men, the

136

officer whose name is still generally unknown in European governmental circles, and the statesman already celebrated but the problem child of the British Government, realized that it was essential to break the stalemate in the West, where the armies were bogged down in the mud, and to follow the sun to the East. Churchill understood that the Dardanelles should be made the objective, and that it was quite feasible to bring weight to bear on the Bosporus and to land troops on the plain of the Danube, follow its course from the mouth to Vienna, and win over all the Christian peoples of the Balkans. The centuries-old foundations of Austria, the ostensible cause of the conflict, were cracking. She would welcome an Allied victory as a liberation which would allow her to throw off the yoke of Prussia, under which she had been groaning ever since Sadowa. But this project was obstructed by the hostile attitude of those who understood neither Shakespeare nor Winston Churchill, nor the fact that the fatal day of May 5, 1453, when Constantinople fell, was a great tragedy for civilized Europe.

The War Office and the High Command were hostile to the prophet who presided over the Admiralty; in France this idea, this stroke of genius, was met with criticism and skepticism by the traditional allies of the Turks ever since Francis I—an alliance which was renewed by Pierre Loti. The Dardanelles, Gallipoli, were half measures foredoomed to failure, which could have been avoided by the rapid and concerted action which Churchill advocated. If his advice had been followed, it would have taken the Allies two years less to achieve victory.

137

All the blood which saturated the fields of France between 1915 and 1918 need not have been shed. And Churchill, the prophet, went into the political desert, his prophecies guarded in his heart until the next war.

From 1916 to 1917 Churchill was fighting in Flanders. Once more he put on the uniform which he had not worn for fifteen years and the curtain of silence falls. . . . But not for long! Colonel C. B. Thomson, author of the secret report advocating the Eastern front, became a Brigadier-General and took part in the campaign in Palestine, including the siege of Jericho. Instead of taking Constantinople, he entered Jerusalem with General Allenby's troops. Churchill and Thomson met again in London after the war and found themselves in opposite political camps. After retiring from the army, Thomson joined the Labour Party and was Ramsay Macdonald's principal adviser when he became Prime Minister. Later as Lord Thomson he became Air Minister and died in France, in the R. 101 airship disaster. Churchill again became a member of the Cabinet in Stanley Baldwin's Government. Both Churchill and Thomson bear the same scar of a wound to their pride in that they were not able to persuade those responsible for policy in the 1914-18 war to take the only possible action which could have enabled Europe to regain its lost unity.

Churchill's prophecies earned him the usual fate of prophets, who, if they are not killed, are stoned—at least that was the ancient custom. Between the two wars, he did not stop denouncing the two-headed hydra, the double dictatorship so firmly in the saddle both in the Kremlin and in Munich. This was the beginning of those eleven years which were almost unbearable for a man of Churchill's character and urge to action. He saw clearly what was happening. His was a lone voice in the desert, warning Ilion that her walls were about to fall. He realized that every vote in Parliament brought the grim future for England one step nearer. He refused to vote, whether the Conservatives or the Socialists were in power. There was no further question, alas, of the Liberals—the party to which he belonged in his youth. Asquith, who had been his Prime Minister and whose confidence he had enjoyed, was dead, and Lloyd George had precipitated the inevitable fate of the Party by his disloyalty to his old chief. England now had only two parties destined to succeed each other in office. When the storm, prophesied by Churchill, finally burst, the privilege of forming a National Government was given to Ramsay Macdonald, the pacifist and sincere idealist, whose very mistakes were permeated with nobility of sentiment. Ironically the initials at the bottom of the ministerial declaration of 1933, demanding the rearmament of England, are J.R.M. and not W.S.C. But the reader of Balzac would be justified in saying about all these belated measures, in England as in France: "Too late, my beloved, says Paquita as she lies a-dying."

In the minds of those men who were ignorant of the tragedy about to overwhelm them, Churchill had become the "warmonger." In fact, he was the doctor who is an expert diagnostician and who, because he has the courage to tell his cholera patients that they are suffering from cholera, is accused of infecting them. Actually he is trying to prevent the disease and then when, as always, it is too late, he is left with the task of organizing the treatment. We are at the beginning of the year 1938, and the epidemic is about to break out.

The cyclone which will be called World War II is approaching. The earthquake has started, it has been localized, detected and the epicenter is known and recorded on all the seismographs hidden in the War Office. And what are the mayflies doing? They are dancing. But they are ritual dances and no one is allowed to reproach them for these symbolical movements which are the prelude to the human sacrifice in preparation. One man in England went on prophesying, and it is because of his prophecies that he was kept out of office for nearly eleven years. . . .

The President of the French Republic and Madame Lebrun were in London as the guests of King George VI and Queen Elizabeth. The organizer of the festivities in honor of France was Sir Philip Sassoon, our host at Lympne, when Winston Churchill, Frank Hodges, and I gathered under his roof in 1926, when the general strike was threatening the peace of England. Philip Sassoon was now First Commissioner of Works in a National Ministry presided over by Neville Chamberlain. The holder of this office would have been called the Superintendent of Fine Arts in France during the reign of Louis XV. His taste was impeccable. He had spent his childhood and youth amidst famous collections, and was familiar with all the great museums in the world. He himself has collected a large number of priceless works of art, which he lent with great generosity, including even some of his own furniture, to adorn the festivities which were to last for three days. He wanted them to be memorable and worthy of England when she was acting as host to France. When the British Government issued an official invitation to the President and Madame Lebrun to attend Westminster Hall and listen to an oration by the Lord Chancellor, we should see them seated on the famous Louis XIV armchairs covered with Spanish velvet against a background of gold. The value of these chairs was explained to the wife of one of the Cabinet Ministers, who had deplored, in a soft voice, that the Government had not been able to find anything better in the way of seats of honor than these "moldy old chairs"!

When the Covent Garden Opera House was decorated for the gala performance, sprays of lilies were everywhere, on the stage, on the columns between the boxes, mingled with bouquets of English roses. His friends teased Philip about this orgy of flowers, which delighted me. They pointed out that the floral emblem of the French Republic was not the lily. In fact no one knew what the emblem should be, as the Third Republic had not yet chosen a flower to represent it. Somebody suggested wild poppies, but they are not in season; a few bunches of imperial violets are added in haste. I went to the gala performance with Leonie Leslie, where we had seats in the stalls.

On the way to the Opera, she said to me, "We shall be going in through the red awning, reserved for royalty;

Winston will be in the audience and will come and talk to us during the interval." Her beloved nephew Winston —the little boy, whose holidays were the cause of a dispute between the old Duchess of Marlborough and herself, had remained in her eyes what he had always been: a spoilt child, her favorite. How remote all that seemed, and receded still further into the past, as she spoke to me about Covent Garden as it was in Winston's boyhood.

As is usually the case on these occasions, the main spectacle was in the audience, not on the stage. The program was not very good and I could not help thinking of that other gala performance at Covent Garden, the victory gala in 1919, shortly after the signature of the Treaty of Versailles. I was overwhelmed by premonition. Both national anthems were played. On my feet, like the rest of the audience, I could see President Lebrun standing between the King and Queen, both wearing the broad ribbon of the Legion of Honour, the Order founded by the Corsican Bonaparte whom England had fought for twenty years, then admired, studied, loved and glorified like a hero of antiquity—after he had been sent to St. Helena. Suddenly these lines from a poem of Malherbe came into my mind:

> Time will put an end to all those
> Sad memories and you shall have roses
> More than even you can gather . . .

On the way to Covent Garden I had told Leonie about an incident which, though apparently insignificant, had made a great impression on me. I had been invited to

Hythe by Malcolm Macdonald, then Colonial Secretary in Neville Chamberlain's National Government. The chauffeur who was driving me to Hythe was a man whom I had known for many years. I am bound by ties of close friendship with James Ramsay Macdonald's children, a friendship which had originated in connection with the tragic death of our mutual friend, Lord Thomson, which had made me feel closer to the Socialist Prime Minister, who became the head of a national government a few years later. This same chauffeur had often driven me from Chequers, the official country seat of British Prime Ministers, to London and from Downing Street to my hotel. He was very devoted to his old master's family. He had taken part more than once in Ramsay Macdonald's election campaigns. Young Macdonald had taken him into his service after his father's death. He had helped Malcolm during his recent electioneering in Scotland, where his opponent for the vacant seat was young Randolph Churchill, Winston's only son. Randolph had been defeated and Malcolm had triumphed. For this reason and others, due to their opposing political beliefs, there was not much love lost between the Churchills and the Macdonalds. The same, of course, applied to the family servants. These were the facts of the case and nothing could be done about it.

Lord Thomson, whose admiration for Winston Churchill had been unbounded and dated from the time when the two men had conceived together the plan for an Eastern front as the only means of shortening the war, was dead. Their profound attachment to each other was even

143

older in origin, and dated back to the war in the Transvaal. The only Socialist Minister who could have reconciled Churchill and Macdonald was dead and with him had died the bold gesture—Constantinople captured, the Straits open to the English and French fleets, the plain of the Danube overrun as far as Vienna. . . .

These dreams and others flitted through my head on the road from Hythe to London, as I was driven back alone by Ramsay Macdonald's old chauffeur. He expressed to me his anxiety about the situation in Europe in general and about my poor country in particular. The morning papers had mentioned the danger of a simultaneous Nazi invasion of Poland and Romania. Like all self-respecting Scotsmen, the good man was anything but loquacious; it had taken me a good many years to gain his confidence by a few words, a few smiles and long comfortable silences. I agreed with him and then, seeing that I kept silent about the probable misfortunes which threatened my distant country, he continued: "There is only one man in the world who can stop Hitler. We must have Churchill."

I found these words extremely significant. I knew that this man was loyal and faithful to the son of his master, whom he now served, respected and loved as he had loved the father. He was well aware of the fundamental divergence of opinion between Macdonald and Churchill. Besides, he had had every opportunity for arriving at a considered opinion and also the right to express it, as he was a voter. His instinct had dictated those words, that marvelous political instinct which arouses the whole people as a single man in Britain when it is a question of "saving the King." He obviously felt that the storm was about to burst.

I told Leonie Leslie this story as we were driving to Covent Garden—more in jest than in earnest, though she rarely rose to my bait, as her judgment was exceptionally sound and she was a good conductor of political electricity in London society. I used to say to her often, "When will your beloved nephew become Prime Minister?"— "Never," was her invariable reply, "except in the event of a catastrophe!"

That night, in the brilliantly illuminated Covent Garden Opera House, catastrophe was in the air. Winston Churchill came to talk to us in the interval, as Leonie had promised. His bulldog neck bulged out of the gold-embroidered collar of his Privy Councillor's uniform. Flaunting his military orders, pinned over his heart, Winston pushed his way through the dense crowd to come and sit between Leonie and myself for a few moments. I would not say that he looked worried. On the contrary, he looked like an antidote to other people's worries. His face, pale in his youth, now pale pink, had become with time as round as a pearl; his hair, once red, was now nothing but a light down, like that on the head of a newborn baby; his high-domed forehead, the shape of the world map in the form of a globe, lit from within by his luminous thoughts, seemed to be meditating about the approaching end of our present world, not manifesting any great regret. Everything about him was prodigiously different from other men. This is what made everybody recognize him at once, even in this orgy of men in uniform, all dressed as decoratively and conspicuously as he was. The crowd opened to let him pass, as if he alone, the actor, enjoyed some mysterious priority. He came toward us, rolling a little, like a sailor or a young child, as if carried along by an invisible swell, his back rounded, braced to meet a breaking wave, a broadside, a shower of bullets or a stream of stars. He sat down for a moment and embarked without any preamble on the subject uppermost in his mind: "We shall have war. . . . The British Empire will go bang . . . and I . . . and I . . . well, I feel twenty years younger!" He shook himself cheerfully, like a dog who has just come out of the water, and returned to his seat as the curtain rose.

THE COURAGE OF HIS OPINIONS

THIS for me takes first place among all his forms of courage, even if he alters his opinion, as the development of events dictates, which in fact does not often happen. Should we attribute the uncompromising manner in which the young Churchill—become the old Churchill without ever losing the fundamental characteristics of youth—expresses his views to what a French moralist calls "the aristocratic delight in displeasing"? It is true that he has always persisted in saying what he thinks, and even what he is going to think in the future, without concerning himself overmuch about what others will think about his views, or even about what it may have pleased him to think on a previous occasion. There is no doubt about his taking great pleasure in displeasing; everything he has been, everything he has done, he has done with all his heart, with what is called great zest, even down to waging war.

It would be foolish to claim that he wanted William II to be what he was, and the same applies with even greater force to William's direct successor, Hitler. But as these men existed, have existed in the past and will exist again in the future, he was convinced that the German people, led like a docile flock by these insane shepherds, should be led back from defeat to reason. And that was to be his special task: he did not make war; he had to wage a war already declared. His job was to win it, and then it would be for others to disentangle the tangled skein of misfortune, the net into which Aeschylus makes Agamemnon fall on his return from the Trojan War. For such an enterprise, enthusiasm is at least as necessary as new weapons. Once one has started on a certain course of action, to finish it successfully one has to throw oneself into it with enthusiasm and love. There is no escaping from this dilemma; you cannot hunt wolves with lapdogs. When William II was smitten with the mad idea of invading Belgium because he was incensed with France and Russia, all England was aroused. Opinions had been profoundly divided as to the war, but now all rallied without hesitation around the Liberal banner, raised on high by Asquith. And then Winston Churchill rushed to Downing Street for confirmation of the news that German troops had invaded neutral territory guaranteed by the signature of Germany.

Churchill had long realized not only that the war was inevitable, but that it was a righteous war which it was the duty of England to wage in the interests of mankind. Churchill was proud to be associated with plans for defeating an adversary who was arrogantly certain of victory and who, like a man going off to shoot a lion, lost his chance by killing a dove on the way. William II, the Emperor of Germany, had thought himself clever, but he had succeeded in revolting the conscience of all decent men. The celestial hosts are man's most valuable allies in those countries in which people's minds have been steeped in the religious spirit, biblical and evangelical, for so many centuries. We have seen it in the case of the *Lusitania*, ever since Salamis, since Constantine and since Clovis, and the Germans will learn it, without understanding it, first at Rethondes and then at Rheims, on May 5, 1945, twice in less than thirty years. Churchill never fails to take advantage of his adversary's mistakes. When Rudolph Hess, the most important person in Nazi Germany after Hitler, whose deputy he was, took a plane and set off for Scotland in order to offer a separate peace for England to the Duke of Hamilton what was Churchill's opinion of this extraordinary attempt? He will express it in six words: "The worm is in the apple." This was his opinion from 1941 onward.

Again, it required courage to take the first step toward meeting Stalin, his old enemy, and to shake the hand of Molotov, which signed the Ribbentrop agreement when England was at death's door; to seek out his congenital enemy in his own lair, in Moscow, when the Germans are barely a few hundred kilometers from the Kremlin; and there to defend himself against the strategy and sarcasm of the master of all the Russias. At the dinner table, Stalin upbraided him for attacks on him in the press. Churchill retracted nothing; he simply said to his ally, Marshal Stalin: "That was when you were against us."

Churchill knew how to make the Labour members of his own War Cabinet, who were helping him save England, adhere to the spirit as well as the letter of the Party truce. He kept his own feelings in check, for as long as it proved expedient. His natural courtesy, instead of a policy of hammer blows which, in ordinary life, he is more apt to deal his friends than his political enemies, allowed him to preserve the unity which must prevail in the Cabinet at all costs until the war had been won. But here again, the courage of his opinions did not forsake him, and if he damped down the fire, that does not mean that the fire was out.

He gave us a striking demonstration of it once more after his defeat at the hands of the British electorate, as if with the express object of making him seem even greater to posterity. This was the time when the new Socialist measures, marked first by the nationalization of the railways, then the nationalization of the mines, were threatening England's key industry—the steel industry. Churchill expressed his opinion in a form in which comedy vies with tragedy, according to the formula with which Shakespeare created his Caliban. Somebody was arguing in Churchill's presence about who deserved the credit for being the real founder of the Labour Movement in England; between two puffs of his cigar, Churchill muttered a name which was not the one his audience expected:

"Christopher Columbus."

His hearers thought hard, trying to detect his line of reasoning, and one of them protested: "Christopher Columbus? Why?"

"Because," replied Churchill, imperturbably, "when he started, Christopher Columbus did not know where he

150

was going; when he arrived, he did not know where he was . . . And he did it all with other people's money!"

Having at his defeat in the 1945 election regained his liberty, which has never been hampered except by limits imposed by his own mood—relieved of the burden, back with his favorite studies, what would he do with his time? As Prime Minister at the height of the struggle he qualified for Marshal Joffre's immortal statement: "I do not know who won the Battle of the Marne, but what I do know is that if it had been lost, it would not have been my fault!" The same applied to Churchill and the Battle of England. When the storm was over, the Government which he led with such a firm hand fell into other hands. What would he do? Cincinnatus' plow will naturally be proposed by his adversaries, but we know that classical studies were never his strong point—that blank page of Latin translation, now legendary, does not suggest that he would welcome a return to rustic life. Protected by the fiction of his irresponsibility, this man of seventy behaved like the young man in the *Education Sentimentale*: "He traveled. He knew the melancholy of steamboats, the chill dawn under a tent, the bewilderment of too much scenery and too many ruins, the bitterness of interrupted friendships . . ."

That popularity which had buoyed him up throughout the war had receded; it was now coming back through other channels; he had been in office too often and he knew his Shakespeare too well to waste time in vain re-

151

grets. "Live Brutus. . . . Let him be Caesar!" The mob
is mad, but it is also wise; the greatness of a people can
be measured by the yardstick of its ingratitude, the people of Athens in its heyday were like that and the Roman
people; and the French denied Clemenceau the Presi-
dency of the Republic, after having nicknamed him "The
Father of Victory." In just the same way, the British people demobilized Churchill without even waiting for general demobilization. He might have been carried away by
bitterness, but not at all! He took the blow in his usual
manner, superbly. He knew that he was quite capable of
overcoming temporary misfortune—in fact, created for
that very purpose. He would appear in procession in the
streets of London on victory day. He drove to the official
platform in an open carriage modestly drawn by two
horses, sitting by the side of his political opponent—he
on the left, and his opponent on his right, as protocol
would have it. And who would seem to be less triumphant
then than Mr. Attlee, on that day Prime Minister and
leader of the Labour Party with a crushing majority in
Parliament? It is true that at the hour of mortal danger,
Churchill himself appointed Attlee deputy Prime Minister, with a seat in the Cabinet. The idea of a National
Government inaugurated at his expense by the Socialist,
Ramsay Macdonald, in 1931, remained a good one until
the war had been won. But afterwards the time had come
to accept defeat, in exchange for victory, from the hands
of the electorate—from the hands of the English people
which owed their salvation to him.

No doubt, there were illustrious precedents which he

might invoke to help him withstand the ordeal of being abandoned and ignored by the great public, most unjustly according to all criteria of human gratitude and reason. He has seen Asquith deprived of his high office by the treachery of Lloyd George, whom he had saved from the dishonor of refusing to serve England when dire danger threatened on August 3, 1914. He has seen Asquith, that great parliamentarian and servant of the nation, abandoned by all his ministerial colleagues, twice defeated at general elections, not even able to retain his seat in that Parliament which he had glorified by his incomparable eloquence during the course of a quarter of a century. He had seen him refusing to accept the honors which the Sovereign is in the habit of bestowing on those whom public favor has deserted after the fight has been won—which is almost always the rule. He has seen him bear popular ingratitude with serenity.

This is the place for me to record an experience which allowed me to measure both the wisdom and grandeur of British institutions, as well as their absurdity in the eyes of other nations. I was, at the time when Churchill was defeated at the elections, at the other end of Europe, practicing the profession of a journalist in the capacity of correspondent for the foreign press. I was then employed by a French paper, the *Indépendance Roumaine.*

Hence, it was my privilege to be the only woman present at the weekly conference of the war correspondents representing the foreign press, and to form an opinion as to the importance of present and future events. I wrote one article a week, carefully limited to my personal observations of the V.I.P.s of the day, as I had actually known them. I was induced to write several articles on President Roosevelt, both before and after his death, on President Truman, and on various French and English statesmen. Churchill was then extremely popular in that part of Europe where even an ill-informed public was obscurely conscious of the fact that the fate of Eastern Europe had largely depended upon Churchill, who had acted as their best and most intelligent defender. His immense popularity had not yet begun to decline and the articles I wrote about him were appreciated more than any of my other articles by my unknown readers. One day I was in a shop and the salesgirl, when she heard my name, confessed that she was very worried; she had read my articles and that very morning she had heard on the radio that the great Churchill had quarreled with the King of England. How could such a disaster have happened? I asked her to tell me what she had heard on the radio that had alarmed her, and which I assured her was totally unjustified. She explained simply that Mr. Churchill had refused the highest honor that England could offer, which the King wanted to bestow on him. Was such a terrible thing possible? The great Churchill at variance with his King? She added: "You have written such beautiful things about Churchill, which have made us love him. Can you explain this awful misfortune?"

Reading into this young woman's mind and thinking of all those who must be thinking what she was thinking, fearing what she feared, being disillusioned and feeling that their picture of the man who had saved the world by his superhuman courage was being blurred and smirched, I felt angry with myself because I felt incapable of making her understand that what she considered so terrible was a matter of small significance to the English. To them it was merely a symbol of so many other things which were difficult to explain to those who had not made a study of the political history of England, and who observed the habits and customs of that nation which are so curiously different from all others. How could one make a Frenchman understand that if the President of the Republic offered him the Grand Cross of the Legion of Honour, he was at liberty to decline this great honor; or to a Spaniard whose king had offered him the Golden Fleece, or to a Dane to whom the head of the State had offered the White Elephant of Denmark, or to an Italian the Chain of the Annunciation; and the same for the Romanians, the Greeks, and every other European nation without exception?

This thing, which was unthinkable in every other continental country, was not only possible in England, but quite legitimate, for mysterious reasons almost impossible to explain.

I went back home and proceeded to think about the subject of my next article. Fortunately, I still possessed some snapshots which I had taken in the course of my many visits to England. Among them was one of Mr. Asquith, then Earl of Oxford and Asquith, and his granddaughter, Priscilla Bibesco, who was then six years old and in the act of putting a rose in her grandfather's buttonhole, in a garden on the banks of the Thames.

I had this snapshot reproduced at the head of my article: "Portrait of a Man Who Twice Refused the Order of the Garter, Offered to Him by the King of England, and Who Accepted It When It Was Offered for the Third Time." Such is the peculiar character of the great servants of the English nation, that neither the monarch nor his subjects are astonished by this curious custom which allows them to decline an offer of the highest national distinction, without in any way affecting the cordial relationship between the sovereign and his minister or impugning his loyalty to the crown. Churchill, when he refused the Garter for the first time, after his defeat at the 1945 elections, declined it with a witticism which delighted King George VI: "How could I accept the Garter from Your Majesty, when I have just received the boot from the British people?"

How was Churchill going to keep himself occupied during that period which destiny had granted to him between the moment when he was expelled from office and the year in which the British voters would decide that his retirement had lasted for long enough? Once again, it is adversity which will allow us to measure the extent of his true greatness and the quality of his courage. I do not know which to admire most, the political sense of the English people as a whole, or Churchill's particular genius. Never has the code for deciphering political events, which has been handed down to us in a straight line from Greece, demonstrated more clearly the excellence of the method which permits the greatest empire of modern times to survive and to triumph yet again. *Power corrupts human reason,* was a Greek saying. An English humanist and statesman, Lord Acton, ventured to elaborate, with considerable justification: "And absolute power corrupts absolutely." These true words applied to Caesar, to Philip II, to Napoleon, and lower down in the scale, much lower, in our day, to Mussolini and to Hitler, have proved that the essential man, taken as a governing animal, has changed little if at all. Sole and supreme command, an absolute necessity for saving the nation in the hour of its greatest peril, if it is concentrated in the hands of the same man for more than four or five years, invariably leads to the same delusional phenomena of greatness. If the man of genius is removed from office, he can succeed in keeping his sanity; if he is maintained in power by a defective constitution, or by the absence of a constitution, his loss of reason becomes inevitable.

Examples abound throughout history; the case of Stalin, and I would even go so far as to say that of President Roosevelt, both admirable in action at the hour of supreme peril, but both of them maintained by circumstances in power for too long. But the destiny of Churchill, like all great destinies, was a Muse, if we are to believe Chateaubriand who wrote: "Only those destinies are admirable which are subject to great misfortunes." The ingratitude of the English people toward Churchill magnifies his true greatness, whereas if he had been returned to power in 1945 with a majority, however diminished, he could have been unbalanced by his victory. The sadness inseparable from those days which follow hard on victory so well described in *The Trojan Women*—the gray dawn after the taking of Troy—would have overwhelmed a genius with less vigor than that which Churchill manifested all his life. Relieved of power, his spirit reverted in a strange way to the elasticity of youth. As leader of the Opposition—an Opposition reduced to impotence by the very magnitude of the electoral success of his old Labour opponents—his mind was refreshed; he seemed toned up, reinvigorated, exalted by the clear field opened in front of him. His two fellow delegates to Teheran and Yalta, Stalin and Roosevelt, have paid their tribute to human nature. Roosevelt based his reliance upon his sovereign charm, to the extent of believing that he was the only man capable of making Stalin see reason. On his side, Stalin succeeded in acquiring more territory, an altogether disproportionate increase in his empire, and that is precisely its weakness. The Baltic states follow Poland, East Prussia, Czechoslovakia, Hungary, Romania and Bulgaria, all in the wolf's maw, which cannot swallow so many titbits at a single gulp; human reason had completely disappeared by the time the Potsdam meeting was convened without Winston Churchill and also, alas, without France.

Churchill was the first to understand the real significance of what had been happening. His hands were free, thanks to the superior ingratitude of his people. He left for America. Roosevelt was dead and Harry Truman had succeeded him. On March 5, 1946, Churchill delivered his famous speech at Fulton, Missouri.

This speech, printed in full by the press, raised a storm of invective. Very few have understood, but once again he was the first to understand, and to have the courage of his opinions.

At the present time we can well ask why what he said caused such an outburst of rage, seeing that proof is accumulating every day. He was only citing incontrovertible facts, which demonstrated his perspicacity, or what others call his gift of prophecy, and which is merely the manifestation of his genius applied to public affairs. He was merely following the procedure of an artist in any field of creative art; what shocks today invariably becomes what is most admired tomorrow.

At Fulton, Churchill simply put forward the evidence for what has since become common knowledge. His "monumental endurance," as one of his biographers, A. L. Rowse, writes, is only equaled by the flexibility of his imagination, which permits him to face the hard reality of any given situation, and to surround it with a sort of emotional halo which renders the things he says poetic and thus unforgettable. "I do not believe," said Churchill to his Fulton audience, "that Soviet Russia desires war. What they desire is the fruits of war and the indefinite expansion of their power and their doctrines." Speaking as the champion of the West, the guardian of the English-speaking nations who was, at the same time, anxious to save the Russian people—a brave ally in the war against Germany—from the terrible future its present masters might be preparing for it, he pointed to the remedy:

We cannot afford, if we can help it, to work on narrow margins, offering temptations to a trial of strength. . . . If the population of the English-speaking Commonwealth be added to that of the United States with all that such co-operation implies in the air, on the sea, all over the globe, whether in science or industry or in moral force, there will be no quivering, precarious balance of power to offer its temptation to ambition or adventure.

For six years, from 1945 to 1951, the world was able to observe this strange phenomenon of a man who held no office, but who, nevertheless, had far more influence on and wielded far more power over public opinion than those who were actually in power. In reality, during this time of trouble and disturbance which followed the defeat of England's enemies, Churchill had remained the true arbiter of Western opinion. A Danish publicist, Mr. Huizinga, has pointed out that Churchill possessed yet another form of courage, on top of all the others he has already shown, the courage to warn the English public—and he did so as early as November 1945, five months before his Fulton speech—that the leadership of the new system necessary for insuring the safety of Western civilization has passed from England to the United States of America. And the Dane concludes: "Here is a fact which English public opinion, still exalted by the pride of victory and still intoxicated by the heady fumes of success, will have difficulty in accepting. This bitter medicine was administered to this proud nation by the most illustrious of its sons, Churchill himself."

When he uttered his solemn warning at Fulton, Churchill, the great realist beneath his mask of a poetic orator, knew his people well enough to be sure that they would not be discouraged by the fear of being supplanted by the Americans; the Englishman, as A. L. Rowse wisely remarks, is very different from the German in this respect and never wastes his time kicking or protesting against hard facts.

It is of little consequence to Churchill that the balance of power has shifted overseas to that great English-speaking people, which is the most powerful nation in the world today; he is only concerned with watching over the arch saint and he has no reason for indulging in vain regrets. Those transatlantic peoples are our own flesh and blood, modified by geographical factors, by circumstances and by mass migrations from Europe.

Chateaubriand himself, that other visionary, when discussing the America of his day, called it: "The new universe in which humanity is being reborn." Lord Thomson said to me one day: "They talk about forming the United States of Europe, but such an organization already exists! They ask me: What is your evidence, where is it? And I answer: In America, of course!"

And in that same speech at Fulton, Churchill visited by the spirit of prophecy declares: *"It may well happen— and I feel that it is eventually bound to happen to us— because the dangers of the modern world are so frightful, that we shall be obliged to merge with each other; our history as a separate people is at an end and the English-*

speaking nations of the whole world will unite." His infallible instinct tells him that this principle of common citizenship is in the air, and he declares that he is content to leave it to destiny to decide when and where it shall be implemented: "That destiny which is holding its arms out to us," he says, "and which many of us can already imagine."

THE COURAGE TO PAINT

I HAD the opportunity several times, over the years, when I was staying in the country in England, to see Churchill at his easel, either outside in the open or, if he was painting an interior, installed in the corner of a room where no one ventured to disturb him, except perhaps his host and his Aunt Leonie.

The first of these occasions was in the garden at Lympne one May. At the time, Churchill was Chancellor of the Exchequer. He had set up his easel under my window in the first rays of the spring sun and was surrounded by paint boxes, cloths stained with all the colors of the rainbow and paint brushes set in pots, just like the painters on the quays of the Seine. Lady Leslie and I crept up behind him on tiptoe. There we stood for a few moments, still some distance away from him, watching him. He was completely absorbed and seemed unconscious of our presence. He had been painting ever since the early morning, wearing his immense sombrero of light felt which was as faded and frayed as if he had been wearing it ever since he had been fighting in Cuba. He was painting that great expanse of marshland spread out below the cliffs of Folkestone. It was there, according to the legend, that Julius Caesar had landed on these foggy islands where the Romans were hoping to find pearls; this was the view that had inspired Churchill, the artist, patiently concentrating throughout that fine spring morning on an attempt to reproduce the different shades of blue of the sea and the sky, relieved by the yellow tone of the rushes.

Four sketches were drying in the sun, propped up against the feet of the easel. He was now working on the fifth canvas, almost throwing the paint on; he was sighing, practically out of breath with the effort of expressing his feelings. The ringing of a bell to call us to lunch made him raise his head. He caught sight of us and smiled. But there was a characteristically rebellious quirk at the corner of his lips when Leonie Leslie said, half in jest, half seriously, "As you have painted the same landscape five times this morning, and as Marthe is going back to Paris tomorrow, I think you ought to give her one of your sketches so that she can have it put up for sale at the Anglo-French bazaar . . . it is in aid of the British cemeteries in France." Churchill listened intently, and I could already see myself carrying off his signature at the bottom of one of these canvases and getting a good price for it.

Leonie insisted. She was teasing her nephew, as she well knew that he hated parting with his paintings. Winston turned around, seemingly very angry (but the will-o'-the-wisp was dancing in the corner of his eye) and said, slowly and emphasizing each word: "They are too bad to sell and too dear to me to give!"

To feel that he is doing a job of honest manual work plays some part in his love of painting. It is his way of penetrating into the secret of the world. He will go so far in his passion for experience and experiment, in his lonely labors, that he will exchange his palette knife for the mason's trowel. He will build a wall in his garden at Chartwell so that it will catch the light of the sun and the moon, reflect the rain and the color of the weather. He has found yet another way of expressing himself.

"Audacity is an important element in the art of painting," he wrote in a book published after the second World War, which he called *Painting as a Pastime*—his way of passing the time in search of his soul, when he has not been immersed in his major occupation of governing his fellow men, which has so often been granted to him and equally often denied to him.

During a period of thirty-three years, painting has been his Ingres' violin, the only one on which he has not finished playing up to now.

He has always set his face against benefiting from the leniency or even favoritism, which was to be expected when he had become a great man, from the men who were official judges at picture exhibitions. In order to avoid the possibility of having his pictures accepted for the Royal Academy Exhibition of 1945 on any other grounds except pictorial merit, he insisted that his canvases should be submitted to the committee under the name of Mr. Winter. Before sending them in, he asked his friend Sir Edward Marsh, whose well-known taste in the field of painting would be a guarantee of the quality of the paintings which were to be shown, for his candid opinion. It was a delicate matter, but Sir Edward Marsh assured me that it was Mr. Winter himself, "very particular and very determined," who decided to submit only two out of the four canvases which his friend had advised him to exhibit. Of these two, one was "The Blue Sitting-room, Trent Park, 1934." I was visiting Sir Philip Sassoon at Trent Park when Churchill began this painting; it was the last visit I paid to this lovely house, which, like so many others, became a public institution during the war. The time, the place, the circumstances, are perfectly reproduced on this square of canvas, depicting so many admirable things, beloved and very precious, bathed in the blue and gold light in this little room. The treasures of that room—French furniture of the purest Regency style and Chinese art treasures—have since been scattered; who knows in what country they are now, in what antique dealer's showroom, or in what private collector's house? An instant of beauty had gathered them together as if by the wave of a magic wand in the hands of Philip Sassoon. "Stop and stand still, you are so beautiful," Goethe's Faust would have said, speaking to that fugitive moment which is never anything but a fleeting apparition, no sooner seen than vanished. Isolated from the other guests, Winston Churchill had succeeded in capturing this moment and reproducing it on canvas for posterity. In 1949, it was sold in London by auction, at Clementine Churchill's request and for the benefit of the Y.W.C.A., of which she was President, for the sum of 1,250 guineas. The purchaser, the Brazilian senator, François d'Assise Chateaubriand, presented it to the São Paulo Museum, where the present value of the painting is assessed by the insurance company at £13,000. This is one of the very few of his paintings which is signed by his initials W.S.C.

Most of his pictures he has kept himself; he makes no secret of his affection for them, in spite of his highly developed critical sense. He says of himself that he collects his own paintings. I was told the following anecdote about the President of the English Academy in Spain, James Sinton Sleator, who, during a visit to Chartwell, spent part of his time painting at the same time as his host. At the end of his visit, Winston Churchill claimed that he had benefited from watching his guest paint and proposed to pay him a fee proportionate to the skill he had acquired. Sleator categorically refused. But, as a souvenir of the hours of enjoyable hospitality which he had received at Chartwell, he suggested that his so-called "pupil" should give him one of his canvases painted by him during that period. Winston Churchill could not refuse, but he hesitated for a long time.

Sleator, absent-minded like so many artists and notorious for the disorder in which he lived, forgot to take the canvas away. When he discovered his omission, and though he loathed writing letters, he wrote to his host asking for the canvas which he had forgotten to take. The reply was friendly but very firm; as he had not taken the trouble to take the painting away with him, it was obvious that he could not have attached much importance to it. Hence, the canvas remained in Churchill's possession.

The Royal Academy of 1947 was the last at which his canvases were exhibited under the name of Mr. Winter.

His painting career then became official, as he was unanimously elected an Honorary Academician Extraordinary. This gave him the right, in common with all the other members of the Academy, to exhibit six pictures in 1951. But in 1952, as he had become Prime Minister once again, he was not able to exhibit more than four canvases.

In a competition for contemporary English humorists, among whom figure such shining lights as Hilaire Belloc, Noel Coward, and Aneurin Bevan, a motion was voted to recognize the mastery of Churchill in the fertile field of British humor. It stated, SIR WINSTON CHURCHILL *who at all times, in all circumstances, in any company, on any subject, without ever committing the slightest fault against taste or tact, can make everybody laugh.*

What greater praise could any man wish for?

It was an open secret in London: the official portrait presented to Sir Winston Churchill for his eightieth birthday was not to his liking. The donors' intention was good, but the portrait painter was no genius. The color of the hands was so unlike that of the model that when he was first shown his likeness in the painter's studio, he hurried across the room, picked up a brush and changed the color of the hands in less time than it has taken me to write these words.

Iconographic representations of Sir Winston Churchill are few, in spite of his immense popularity. There are far more caricatures of him than there are portraits.

It will not be necessary, therefore, for his future admirers to vie with one another for a picture of him, as happened in the dictator countries and even in Egypt where the Pharaohs scratched the scrolls of their predecessors. The deification of great men in England is limited to a few statues and a few busts. Winston Churchill already has his portrait, given by the nation, one single portrait and not one of the best at that; soon he will have his statue. But that will not be more than the single specimen, which he unveiled himself recently, of Asquith, the Prime Minister under whom he served, such is his fidelity to the memory of the old Liberal leader who appointed him to his first Cabinet post. It must be noted that the courage to be duly grateful is to be numbered among his other rare forms of courage.

I have never so clearly realized the difference between a dictator and a great man until the day when circumstances caused me to meditate about the proliferation of pictures of a political personality, a phenomenon typical of the basest sort of demagogy, which has manifested itself in our day in the case of Hitler, Stalin and, more recently, Peron and Evita Peron. Churchill's face, so often photographed during the war and of necessity reproduced innumerable times in the press, has never become the obsession which the effigies of the men who thought themselves deified by their peoples became. They were shown on and in all public buildings, in all the stations, and in every house, only to be lacerated later on, destroyed, thrown into the gutter and, worse, totally forgotten for always.

I remember a trifling incident which enlightened me as to the attitude of the English toward their great man—

169

a mixture of loyalty and modesty. There can be no single Englishman who does not realize that of all contemporary statesmen, Churchill alone really saved the nation. And nevertheless, what mutual discretion with regard to his iconography! I was to have a personal demonstration.

I was in Constantinople and was living in a villa isolated in its garden on the shores of Asia in September 1943. One of my friends, a correspondent of the *Times,* knowing a good deal about my life, my opinions and the retreat in which I was determined to live pending the inevitable culmination of the events which concerned my unhappy country, suggested taking me for a car ride, to distract my gloomy thoughts. He told me that the Turks had just finished making a fine road which, skirting the shore of the Bosporus, extended beyond Rouméli-Hissar, as far as the place where one can see the shores of the Black Sea, our Mauro-Thalassa. He thought that it would give me pleasure to contemplate with him, he who had been for a long time his paper's representative in happy Dacia, that sea where the old Ister mingles its waters with the waves of that Euxine bridge so abundantly embellished with memories of Greek mythology.

I gladly accepted his invitation to go for a ride in the countryside dedicated to Iphigenia. An hour before the time appointed for our excursion, this Englishman telephoned me to say that his car had broken down and he could not drive it out of the garage. Would I mind waiting an extra hour while he found another car—or would I prefer to cancel the trip and do something else? I answered that I had nothing else to do and that I was quite content to wait until he was able to fetch me. An hour later, I heard the hooting of a horn and went out to my garden gate. I found the *Times* correspondent at the wheel of a superb car and sat down beside him. And I caught sight, in the place where there is usually a medallion of St. Christopher, the patron saint of car drivers, a tiny photograph of Churchill, which I gazed at with interest.

My companion noticed that I had seen the photograph. He said to me, with a somewhat embarrassed smile: "Oh! You know . . . this car belongs to a Greek. . . ."

THE COURAGE TO STEP DOWN

HERE is another of the Churchillian sayings which is being repeated all over London and was told to me several times, here and there, by people who seem to take pleasure in ferreting out these things. His innumerable friends and admirers never grow tired of repeating his brilliant witticisms. His private physician and friend, Lord Moran, finally made up his mind to tell Churchill that it was time to take it easy. The great man was not pleased and answered, reluctantly, "Very well! I'll do it, if you say so, I'll do it. . . ." Then, raising his voice: "After all, we cannot expect Anthony to live forever!"

It was out of solicitude for his successor, Anthony Eden, who had been designated for a long time, that he made his final bow. He wanted to make way for somebody more mortal than himself . . .

Tonight is a landmark. It is the night of April 16, 1955, the eve of Churchill's resignation. It is as though we had witnessed a sudden change in time, as if between yesterday and today an epoch has changed. Time has crumbled away! Tonight, London-Pompeii is covered in gray ash. I am accompanied back to my hotel by Julian Amery. We have both had supper with some friends, to discuss the great event before the papers come out. Julian is one of the most brilliant of the younger Conservative M.P.s, already excellent potential ministerial material. Just before he left me, he raised his eyes toward the starless sky and said, "They can say what they like!—that we shall have a majority at the next elections, that it is our turn, time for my generation to be given a chance . . . tonight, I only know one thing: Tonight is the end of my youth . . . I shall never have anyone else whom I can wholeheartedly admire!"

Such is Churchill's appeal to the imagination, that this poignant confession was made to me, quite spontaneously, and threw a light on the state of mind of a large number of young men who are about to enter the political arena. What makes the soul of these young Englishmen so responsive to greatness, almost as if they were impregnated with it, so that they prefer it, even when fallen, to their own ambitions? Nostalgically, they watch the great tide receding, fearing that they may have to stay on shore for a very long time before they can set sail again. Anthony Eden, who is not yet sixty, succeeds the octogenarian who has held the center of the world's stage for so many years, and we have this cry from the heart torn from the conscience of one of these young actors who will step onto that stage tomorrow. I had now reached the lobby of my hotel. Few people seem to have gone to bed.

Old acquaintances gather in groups. We are reduced to the spoken word, to oral tradition, as in Homer's time, as the papers have not yet appeared. We hang on the lips of the real initiates—M.P.s young and old, irrespective of their political orientation; each one tells what he has seen or heard, at dinner, or in the House of Commons

173

in the afternoon, when Churchill did not put in an appearance. He was at Buckingham Palace. That is all that I could gather before going up to my room to sleep. I reached the elevator just as the doors closed, so I sat down in the middle of an improvised meeting, in front of the empty grate in the fireplace, in this palace of drafts (which is the best appellation for any public room in an English hotel). We were stirring the burning ashes . . . Sir Alfred B., Conservative M.P., is telling about the scene he has just witnessed. A group of young M.P.'s in the lobby of the House of Commons were bending over that horrible device, the tape machine, which pours out the news so indifferently and which has broken more than one heart. A young Labour M.P., a stranger to the rest of them, had joined the group and was watching the ribbon of paper inch forward with the news that had become common knowledge much earlier. Churchill's resignation was being printed out by the machine; the last words were coming forward; then the last letters and the full stop, to a page which tonight marks a pause in a great destiny—so great that one cannot attempt to measure it without some degree of awe. When the tape had passed over the roller of the machine (which bore a sign asking people not to touch it), and some other news, which interested no one, started on the tape, the members of the group raised their heads and were about to disperse. Then the young Labour M.P. raised his voice and cried: "There! That's finished! You Tories ought to be pleased with yourselves! For it is you, we are all well aware, who have finally succeeded in getting rid of him!" He had spoken in tones of angry despair.

"Yes, it is true," answered one of the young Conservatives as he walked away, "we are responsible, but what we have done, we have done with tears in our eyes!"

We were about to talk about something else; but no; it is impossible at the end of the day chosen by the great man to lay down his burden. The day is a Tuesday which, according to the routine of the Court, is the day for the weekly reception of the Prime Minister by his Sovereign. He has made his usual report to the Queen. Current matters were discussed, some disposed of, others kept for the following week; there were some documents to be signed, some appointments to be made, a few incidents, spread over five continents, to report. At the end, there will be the ceremony of handing in the Seals; it is simple and short. But the Queen has commanded her Prime Minister to arrive at the Palace at five-thirty instead of the usual hour of six. What was the reason for this unprecedented change in the timetable? The Queen was anxious that her children should be present with her and see the great Churchill laying down his burden and taking his leave. Whoever we are, we are all responsible for our children's memories; but the Queen more than anyone else. . . .

In London, history has been made during these two days; yesterday Churchill was in the House of Commons, not in order to take his leave, but to present an important

Bill to Parliament, which, according to custom, had to have two signatures—his own, as Prime Minister, and that of his Minister for Foreign Affairs, Sir Anthony Eden. The Bill was to propose to the House and announce to the country, to the world, that England would join the defense pact, already signed, between Turkey and Iraq. The Bill was put to the vote and officially ratified by yesterday's Prime Minister and tomorrow's. Thus this pact with Turkey and Iraq, formerly an Ottoman province, today an independent kingdom, will bear (another significant event for contemporary diplomatic historians to record) the signature of the man of Gallipoli, the man who wanted, in the 1914 war, to pass through the Dardanelles and take Constantinople.

"Constantinople, never! It is the key to the world!" Napoleon's famous dictum at Erfurt, when he barred the way to Czar Alexander, still resounds in Churchill's ears—Churchill the historian whose favorite hero remains the Corsican "ogre."

But Churchill the politician knows that there are two ways of putting one's hands on a key: taking it or having it given to one. Thanks to their audacity and political astuteness, Queen Victoria and her Prime Minister, Palmerston, were able to arrange to have it given to them, by means of a defensive alliance which brought the English fleet into the Bosporus, sailing in company with Napoleon III's French fleet, all in full sail, except for the little steamboats invented by Mr. Fulton, the English engineer.

When the ink of Churchill's signature has dried on the last motion voted by the House of Commons, on the last day of his tenure of office, historians will perhaps record this last act of his political career; the man who wanted to seize that key in 1915 by force of arms (when those who had it in their possession had allied themselves with England's enemies) is the same man who secured the key in 1955, in the same way as Queen Victoria's Prime Minister had secured it in 1856—by negotiation.

This was the great Churchill's last act of foreign politics, countersigned by his successor, Anthony Eden.

The key of Downing Street lies under the door. It is in this little house, deceptively insignificant in appearance, which has not changed for one hundred and thirty years, that are gathered together, in the words of Chateaubriand, Louis XVIII's ambassador to London, "A few serious men clothed in black; they are the heirs to the Great Moguls and their orders are obeyed to the ends of the earth." Today, tonight, the key of Downing Street has passed into other hands. The same applies to the key of Chequers which will change masters, and to the key which locks the red leather dispatch boxes embossed with the arms of England and the State secrets they contain; the key passes, still warm from contact with one human heart to another. The Prime Minister sleeps with that key suspended around his neck, as a monk sleeps with his scapulary. It must never leave him, as long as he remains in the service of Her Majesty, her first servant, the man responsible before God and before the Crown for the safety of this people, this country, this nation. These three keys, symbols of the highest civil office to which a man born in this island can aspire, have passed tonight from the hands of Churchill into the hands of Eden.

And the young wife, the new mistress of the house, Lady Eden, formerly Clarissa Churchill, succeeds the less young but still beautiful Lady Churchill. The niece sits at the head of the table instead of the aunt; Clarissa, daughter of Jack Churchill, younger brother of the great Churchill, enters Downing Street, enters Chequers, hard on the heels of her uncle, who has just left them. In both families, the luggage had been packed. The trunks had been sent off the day before and the suitcases were ready to go with their owners. The aunt had shown her niece over both houses, in town as well as in the country, and the transfer of tutelary gods and domestic authority was soon accomplished. I know both houses, and I can assure you that it is no mean feat for the mistress of these houses to see that they are well kept, at the same time preserving the appearance of a home, although both are really public monuments.

When Anthony Eden and Clarissa arrived, the keys passed from uncle to nephew. Nepotism is a word which was invented by the Romans, but we have adopted it, seeing that the phenomenon which the word describes is common in all countries, and at all periods of history. Nevertheless, no one could accuse Churchill of nepotism in appointing his successor. His political heir had been chosen at least ten or twelve years before Sir Anthony Eden's second marriage, to Churchill's niece.

For my part, I feel absolutely certain, because of what

I have heard, seen and felt, that the whole community of English-speaking peoples will never forget the great Churchill. As long as there are Englishmen, as long as they speak English, not one of them will be able to forget the man who was the instrument of their salvation, their great lyrical poet, their great tragedian, also their great comedian, their favorite playwright and actor, their all-in-all, in fact, their Shakespeare! I saw the young Tories who had been anxious for his "resignation" weep real tears when it came to the point of his leaving. A Conservative M.P. under forty, Nigel Nicolson, son of Sir Harold Nicolson, the historian of George V's reign, at a meeting of artists and writers at which I was present that night immediately after the event, told this to Randolph Churchill who had just come into the room, causing a marked increase in the emotional tension of those present. Because of his carriage, his pale complexion, his way of burying his neck in his shoulders, he was uncannily reminiscent of the father.

I remembered Randolph at eighteen. He was an impetuous young man and went to America on a lecture tour in order to avoid having to pass examinations in England which bored and irked him. And people who frequented the Churchillian circles of those days in London said, "Poor Winston! Throughout his early years he was known as Randolph Churchill's son; now he has become Randolph Churchill's father!"

While the red carpet is being promptly rolled up after Churchill has left and is equally promptly being unrolled for Eden tomorrow, I am thinking of the distance between the Foreign Office and 10 Downing Street; it is literally just across the road. The road, or rather, street, is modest and quiet, separated from the traffic by a gate and a few steps; only foot passengers can pass through it, as it is a cul-de-sac. At the far end the steps go down to a pavement and, on the other side of the roadway, there is St. James's Park, where there are so many beautiful trees on lovely lawns surrounding the lake, so many flowers and so many aquatic birds—Barbary ducks, mandarin ducks from China, swans, gray cranes, ibis and pelicans descended from those that James I, Mary Stuart's son, fed with his own hands. But the terrible little house keeps her new occupant a prisoner, as she has kept its successive occupants in the past—prisoners of their own office of power. The two brightly polished copper foot-scrapers are there, one on each side of the doormat, but gentlemen have no need of them. Since the invention of asphalt, the streets of London have been cleaned up—not so long ago, as you can tell from Dickens's novels. The copper door-knocker and bell-push are equally brightly polished. The narrow steps of white stone are still the same; as is the doormat, worn by the feet of so many illustrious men of this Old England which lives only for them and by them. It is the country in which the cult of great men is deeply respected, as Chateaubriand remarked somewhat enviously. England knows that no one is irreplaceable, but she recognizes in Churchill the greatest and best of her sons, and furthermore, the one best equipped for the task of governing a nation so great in courage. I have heard

Churchill himself quote one of Shakespeare's immortal lines, which another Englishman, his friend and mine, Sir Edward Marsh, used as an epilogue in conversation:

"Unarm Eros, the long day's work is done."

Acknowledgments

PRINCESS BIBESCO wishes to thank the following authors (or holders of copyright) and publishers for permission to quote from the works listed: Sir Winston Churchill, *Speeches, The Second World War* (Cassell & Company Limited), *Savrola, Painting as a Pastime* (Odhams Press Limited), "Churchill at Harrow" by Sir Gerald Woods Wollaston, and "Churchill's Liberalism" by Lord Simon, from *Churchill by His Contemporaries*, ed. Charles Eade (Hutchinson & Company Limited); Consuelo Vanderbilt Balsan, *The Glitter and the Gold* (William Heinemann Limited); Mrs. George Bambridge, "A St. Helena Lullaby" from *Rewards and Fairies*, by Rudyard Kipling (Macmillan & Company Limited).

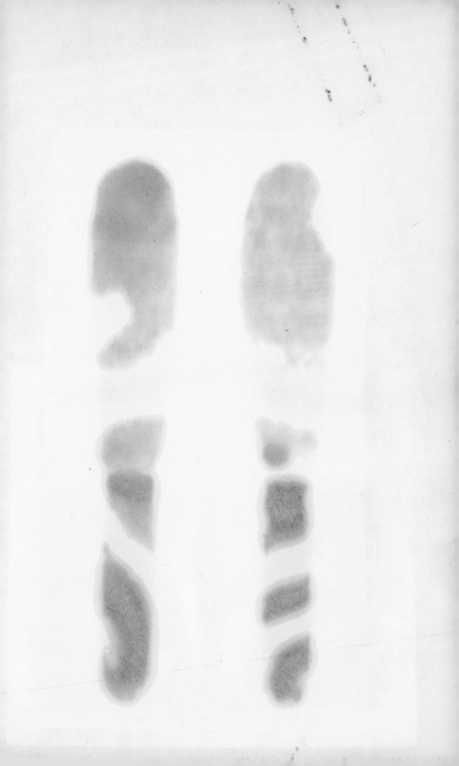